Read Me

A Parental Primer

for "THE TALK"

DR. LANAE ST.JOHN ACS

READ ME
A PARENTAL PRIMER FOR "THE TALK"

DR. LANAE ST.JOHN ACS

Dr. Lanae St.John ACS

Read Me: A Parental Primer for the Talk

Published by: The MamaSutra Publishing

Text and Cover Design by: Soyebo Digital

ISBN-13: 978 1 73241 450 1

To my children, with so much love,
for being the brilliant kids you are and for being patient with my parenting. I look forward to your teen years. Be nice to your mama.
Twokissesandtwohugs!

To the generations that come after us:
I wish all of you passionate, healthy, loving sex lives free of shame, guilt, and stress where you love and are loved deeply in all the ways YOU define it.
Take care and love one another!

Contents

Introduction

It's also important that we educate parents. I think parents would do a good job if we gave them the tools; they don't want to make a mistake with their children and are so scared of doing something wrong they often just don't do anything!

~ Dr. Joycelyn Elders

As a sex educator and mother, the question I am asked most often by parents is, "When should I start talking to my children about sex?" I answer by pointing out these talks are more than just what is done with penises and vaginas. I believe we need to move beyond our traditional thoughts of sex and instead start thinking, "When should I begin talking to my children about *sexuality*?" and that begins right away. Doing this requires a mindset shift and requires a broadening of our understanding of sexuality. Let's think bigger: What are the core concepts that need to be in place for each and every one of us to grow into our happy, healthy adult sexuality? I believe there are five concepts, ones I call "The Five Building Blocks to a Healthy Sexuality," which are Communication, Consent, Respect, Pleasure, and Fantasy. Each of the Five Building Blocks brings to our attention teachable moments that we have every day with our children and can help us focus on what's important instead of what scares us.

I want to challenge you to think differently about why we should consider talking to our kids about sexuality as part of the regular day-to-day, week-to-week routine. Part of our job as parents is to teach our children as many of the important life lessons as we can—and if we cannot teach these lessons directly, we need to make sure our children have the information they need to make smart decisions on their own and to deal with life independently. We can give kids tools to think for themselves, and we have to allow them to be wrong. Consider our own work lives: We all want—or want to be—the manager that gives his/her employees the tools needed to get the job done in the best way possible. The example of a manager who is undesirable is one who either a) micromanages, telling us exactly what to do and how something should be done or b) won't relinquish any tasks or direction to allow growth and learning. Neither of these are optimal. With this book, I propose some ways to help you to be a "good manager" who enables your child's development by giving not only philosophical, abstract, and conceptual advice about human sexuality but also concrete examples that work. With these tips, you can begin to see how the Five Building Blocks can be approached on a day-to-day basis without being overly concerned with what is explicitly done with penises and vaginas.

The first thing that comes to mind when one talks about sex and sexuality is different for everyone. Most people think of "what goes where" during a sexual act. Others think of the feelings they get when the topic is raised; this can be fear, shame, embarrassment, guilt, judgment, or it can be love, joy, fulfilment, happiness, etc. Once we identify our own issues, we can move on to the work that needs to be done to help our children (and maybe even help ourselves in the process).

My approach for how to communicate with kids about sex is that these are conversations that can happen every day and can be easy if you stop thinking about talking about "penises in vaginas." Sexuality is such a broad topic, and lots of folks are scared of it—talking about it, being exposed to it, etc. Understandably! Many of us had terrible information to start—if we got any at all. So, when we are at this point with our children and have no tools or models for how to have these talks, how can we possibly talk to our kids about it? If you can't talk to your partner about sex, I bet you will not be able to talk to your kids about it either. Sex permeates our daily lives in our music, our media, and our own interactions; my blogs at www.themamasutra.net contain great examples for how to use these exposures to talk to your kids about sex.

I think of what I do as "train the trainer" programming: This is less about me teaching your children about "sex" and more about helping you as parents open the lines of communication and create an environment for nonjudgmental, honest, sex-positive attitudes—free of guilt, shame, or taboos. The goal is to create a positive environment for our children to grow into a healthy sex life that is free of guilt or shame. We all want happy, satisfactory sex lives for ourselves. Ultimately, if you look deep down, you probably want this for your children too. That is what I hope this book will do for you.

Me and My Blog

To give you a little bit of background, I am a mom who studied psychology and women's studies in college and who wanted to go on to be a sex therapist. I didn't go back to grad school right away though; as it usually happens, life had a different plan for me. I started a career that I liked, married the man I met in college, moved to New York City, and then relocated to Germany where we started a family.

When both of my daughters were babies, I noticed that the Europeans approached sexuality much differently than Americans. The Germans call the conversation with children about sex "Aufklärung," which means "Enlightenment." I loved that! Experiencing this firsthand as a parent while living overseas brought me back to my original career goal. When my daughters were three and five years old, we moved back to the United States, to San Francisco. About a year or so later, I began my studies at the Institute for Advanced Study of Human Sexuality.

Parenting has given me the opportunity to practice what I preach on the topic of sex education. It's more than practice; I firmly believe my behavior and my approach toward sexuality with my daughters is going to be one that will benefit them and hopefully help them grow up to be happy, sexually healthy adults. The way I am doing this is by giving them open, honest, accurate information. I would much rather have my children come to me instead of using YouTube or Google or some other adult-oriented website to get information about sex.

Most parents refer to the conversation about puberty or sex as "The Talk," which typically contains a brief overview of how babies are made and done in a single conversation. Personally, these topics are something that I take the opportunity to discuss with them whenever they pop up . . . but likely not in the way you would expect. We discuss a TV show, an advertisement on the street, even a joke we hear that touches on the topic of sexuality. I've been continually surprised at how much both of my daughters understand exactly what is going on. I hope this book will show you that children are incredibly curious and ask really good questions when this first starts to become a topic of interest for them.

I consider myself fortunate to have studied human sexual behavior as deeply as one does at the institute at the beginning of my experience as a mother. Sex and parenting are two things that are inextricably connected. In my own personal life, every day I am the sex educator for my children. I strive to provide you with some insight, tips, and techniques to approach this topic in an accessible manner so you can do the same for your kids in a confident way. Everyone deserves to learn about sexuality, and I support you as you talk to your loved ones. Hopefully, you will see how natural (and funny) this topic can be.

A Note

Throughout this book, you will find many of the examples and anecdotes I wrote originally on my blog that I hope serve to further illustrate the subject. Some of the stories have been edited for better pace, but most of the information in this book is new and has not been offered by me online or anywhere else. You will recognize these blogs for three reasons:

1. They will be in a different font.

2. The "voice" is more casual and conversational.

3. Sometimes there is a reference to the age or grade one of my kids was in when the blog was written.

One sample of a blog follows. This was the first one I wrote:

The Bullet

This is when my writing and teaching about sexuality all started:

I was brushing my teeth in the bathroom one morning during my first trimester of grad school. In walked my then seven-year-old Marcia. She was bored because she was ready for school, and she was looking for something to pass the time. She absentmindedly opened a drawer where the hairbrushes were and saw my bullet vibrator.

I always clean my toys, and I didn't have a chance to put this one away where it belonged. The bullet was red and shiny and looked like a lipstick, so she picked it up and said, "Mom. What's this?"

Me: (with a mouthful of toothpaste) "It's nothing. Put it away."

Her: (fiddling with it in her hands) "No, what is it?"

Now, this is the moment I'd been waiting for as a parent and as a student of sexology. I spat out my toothpaste.

Me: (with a big sigh) "It's a vibrator."

Her: (not missing a beat) "What's it for?" By this time, she's figured out how to turn it ON . . .

Me: "It's for your private parts."

Now she is running the little bullet along her nose, over her eyebrows, and along her forehead, a little "d-d-d-d-d-d-d-d" noise from the bullet as it goes.

Her: "It tickles."

Me: "Imagine what it feels like on your private parts."

She neatly turned it off, put it back in the drawer, closed the drawer, and walked out of the bathroom.

I had to laugh at that whole interaction. It was brief. The information I gave was accurate. I could have made up some story about what it was, but I looked at it this way: children figure out at a very early age that adults are full of it. When a parent says, "Don't run or you'll fall!" and the child runs and doesn't fall, there's a little message they get from that. Add to that the numerous times a parent exaggerates a situation with nonexistent consequences and the child figures out it wasn't true. I once read that the more warnings you give a child that don't turn out to be true, the more likely your child is to ignore your advice. Why? Because you obviously don't know what you're talking about. See? Parents can be seen as lousy sources. So why not be truthful?

Some dads (yes, dads—not any moms yet) to whom I've explained my bullet story get sort of bothered that I told my daughter the truth. They ask, "Aren't you afraid of her going off and trying to find it again and use it on herself?" No, not really. She showed me her interest when she turned it off and put it away. Also, so what if she did decide to look for the little bullet vibrator again? I would much rather my daughter understand her own body and what feels good to her than for her to never learn that lesson and expect that someone else is supposed to make her feel good. I think that also explains why there is a difference in the reaction between moms and dads to this story. I am also certain that she got a very clear message from me that I was going to tell her the truth, whether it was embarrassing or not.

Years later, that situation set a really great precedent for the communication between me and my daughter. The ease of interaction in this example, once I let go of my shame and embarrassment about the toy and the subject matter, became apparent to me and ultimately laid the foundation for this book, ***Read Me: A Parental Primer for "The Talk."***

PLISSIT

When developing this book, an approach by one of my favorite sex researchers sprang to mind: Dr. Jack Annon who developed the PLISSIT Model for Sex Therapy. I use all but the last portion of his model in my approach to sex education.

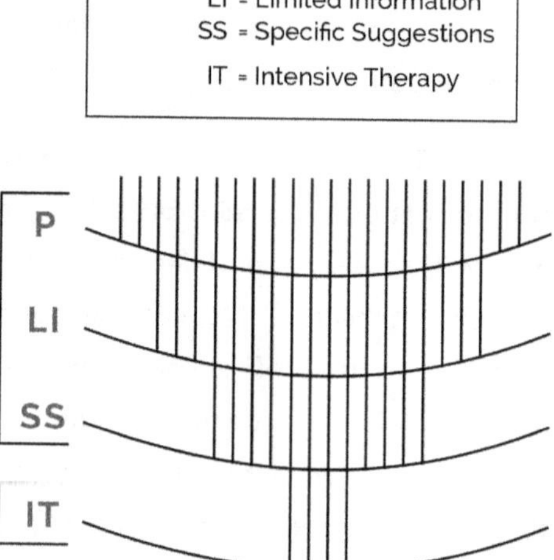

The PLISSIT Model of Sex Therapy developed by Jack Annon

Most people just want to know that they are "normal," and the Permission step gives them the go-ahead or approval to begin to feel comfortable with the subject matter or to seek more help if they are interested. Limited Information would be the next step, providing additional detail about the subject in which they are interested, perhaps facts about anatomy or basic information about how things work. My blogs often function as Specific Suggestions, the next step after providing limited information. IT stands for Intensive Therapy and is where I would refer to a licensed psychologist or other medical professional who could help with any deeper issue or concern. Dr. Annon's model, if appropriately applied, functions like a sieve—only a relative few people would need the IT portion because they likely would have been helped by one or more of the preceding three elements, so I don't include it in my approach.

This book is written with this model in mind. It is my life's work thus far; I hope you find it easy to read, accessible, and helpful in preparing your kids for the modern world.

The Status Quo

Life in Lubbock, Texas, taught me two things: One is that God loves you and you're going to burn in hell. The other is that sex is the most awful, filthy thing on earth, and you should save it for someone you love.

~ Butch Hancock

Why do we avoid talking to our children about human sexuality when it is such an important aspect of our lives? I have spent time talking to many current and aspiring parents, even grandparents. Those conversations were the inspiration for writing this book. The five main reasons I hear from them as to why they don't talk to their children about sex and sexuality are the following:

1. Someone Else Will Do It

Often parents believe that the other parent will have "the talk" with their child. In many instances, this is presumed and never discussed between the parents. One parent may assume that the other parent will talk to the child, but then the other parent might think this is not their role in the relationship. Or a parent wants to give the responsibility to have these conversations to another adult in the family, but then the ball gets dropped. In the end, no one talks to the child.

Other parents presume it is the responsibility of the school to talk to their children about sex. Some parents think once the school has taken this over, it is essentially "taken off the table" for them. But in waiting for school to start the talks (this varies but is usually around fifth grade), parents are assuming incorrectly that the school knows best and that when they start sex education or puberty education in school that must mean it is age-appropriate to do so. In reality, it must start much sooner. Today, 10 percent of American girls will have started puberty before the age of eight[1]. Strangely enough, a lot of parents object completely to the notion that the school should educate their kids about sex. They opt out for their children when the subject is to be taught. Maybe your mind conjures scenes of teenagers engaging in actual sexual activity as homework, but homework for sexuality class can actually comprise lots of different things, none of which is related to actual sex acts. I will talk more about that later when we talk about another building block, *respect*.

Some parents want the church elders to have these conversations for them. The idea here is that parents want their children to learn from a respected source. In most cases though, the source is completely uninformed about human sexual behavior and as a result, the information the children receive is missing a lot of important details; lots of the information can be based on belief or conviction without any science or facts behind them. The child will become misinformed, or at best, underinformed.

Then there are a few people who believe no one should have these talks—that children will figure it out on their own at the right time for them. Of course, this is not a good idea. Frankly, I would never want my own child to be so uninformed (and vulnerable) in this hypersexualized society without a guide or a little navigation.

One point I want to make relates to parenting experts like Susan Patton, The Princeton Mom, who said this in a *Daily Show* segment[2]: "I think sex education in schools, at any grade frankly, I am opposed to. Sex education is something that should be taught by parents to their children. They're not experts, but they can speak to their own experience." While I agree with her on the second and third sentences of that statement, her position in the first sentence fails to acknowledge that most adults don't have a good base of knowledge about sex in the first place. I also recognize that lots of parents are busy. Schedules fill up. Sitting down to talk about something they may not feel informed enough to answer all potential questions doesn't become a priority. This is where schools can come in, provided they have knowledgeable and qualified experts trained in human sexuality who can present the information to the students. But unfortunately, this often doesn't happen.

In that same *Daily Show* segment[3], Ms. Patton went on to say, "If it's that awkward for parents to talk to their children about sexual behavior, then you have to find a website, sit your child down in front of it, and say 'google it, look it up online.'" And here her approach and mine split as well--I do not recommend free-form Google searches for any topic related to sex. Many people go to Google for quick answers on subjects they seek. Children are no different, but their questions, when they are about sex, are ones where Google is NOT the best resource. Alternatively, children are turning to adult video (a.k.a. porn) because they don't like the sex education they are getting and expect to learn something from porn. The downside is that porn is not intended to be used as sex education. It is primarily created for arousal. Children are not alone in seeking out adult video as a sex education resource; I know plenty of adults who use it for this as well.

2. I Don't Want to Be First

There can be significant pressure from other parents around talking to children about sex. A very vocal minority has been known to speak up and put other parents down if they share accurate and honest feedback with their children. Sometimes parents don't talk to their children just out of simple fear that another parent will shame them for being so open ("I can't believe you said that! You should have made something up!"). We are very social creatures, and the mere threat of this public shaming is enough to keep lots of parents silent. What is the result? The message that is received is this: no one should talk about sex openly and honestly. That can't be further from the truth. Many people benefit from speaking up and supporting each other in the face of opposition. Don't let others shame you if you know what you are saying is true. We would not have made the advances we have so far in our social structures if a few people weren't willing to speak out and stand up for what is true and correct.

Another version of this is a fear that our children will reveal to others what we have told them. In other words, "What if I talk to my child first and then they tell other children?" This goes right along with the fear of reprisal. Whether it's real or merely perceived, lots of parents are afraid of what other parents will say if those children hear about sex from their own child. In fact, many times parents won't answer a child's question because they are distracted and want to know the source of the information instead of answering the question. This is different from lying to our kids about Santa

Claus. Lying about the existence of Santa when children are little is a little lie we tell to control their behavior. But it's not necessarily a one-to-one correlation. Lying about Santa won't have the impact of putting their lives in danger (STIs) or affecting the rest of their lives (e.g., an unwanted pregnancy).

3. I'm Waiting for the "Right Time"

Children don't come with instructions that tell a parent what to say at which age. Combine that with our busy schedules and uncertainty about what to say, and it's easy to avoid the topic or put off the conversation altogether.

I liken this to trying to time the perfect storm. When the topic is covered in their elementary and middle schools, the administrators are assuming the children are emotionally, psychologically, or otherwise developmentally ready to hear what the instructor has to say. When it is finally covered in class, some kids just aren't ready to hear about the topic, so they tune it out. Other students question the instructors and their trustworthiness, and they doubt their authority. Some other kids think the teacher doesn't have any idea what they're talking about, so they don't listen. Still others think they know more about human sexuality than the teacher and so they tune out as well. All in all, it's possibly a wasted lesson because it was crammed into a time when the children really weren't ready to listen.

There isn't a prescribed "right time" or best time to have these conversations with your child. NO child is the same in terms of emotional or psychological readiness or maturity level for the conversations about sex and sexuality. Most parents know their own children better than any teacher, and when they are conscious of what is happening in their child's life, they can respond with what is best. You also don't have to worry about making mistakes the first time around because if you are talking about the subject more than once, you get to circle back and correct yourself.

4. I Don't Want to Acknowledge That My Child Is a Sexual Being

There is a tremendous social stigma around sex in general and even more so as it relates to children. Many adults fear that children are inherently sexual beings (which they are) and therefore deny any sexuality to the child.

Our children are growing up every day. Some parents want to avoid thinking about this because they don't want to deal with their kids getting into "trouble"—trouble being pregnancy, sexually transmitted diseases, fears that their children will be taken advantage of, reputation concerns, and not being mature enough to handle this topic. It also brings up a realization of our own aging and mortality.

Sometimes it's difficult to acknowledge that our children are sexual beings because it means we have to accept that we as parents are sexual beings as well. For some adults, it's even more difficult to acknowledge that our own parents are (note present tense use) sexual beings. If our aging parents are still around, chances are they are still sexual after all these years. Yes, plenty of seventy- and eighty-year-olds still have very enjoyable sex. I suspect that when you get to that age you are going to want to continue to be a sexual being as well.

This knowledge about sex and sexuality will come in handy throughout one's lifetime. If you tell your child "just don't have sex," most children will want to know why. Being able to say why in full detail (instead of just "because I said so") will be easier for your child to hear and process.

5. I Don't Know What to Say or My Child Seems to Know Already

Many adults didn't get any information regarding sex from their own parents, caregivers, teachers, etc. Others got some information, but they later found out (sometimes the hard way) that the information was incorrect, or at best, misleading. Sometimes it is simply embarrassment that prevents us from talking openly. Whatever the root cause, the dilemma is the same: How do we talk to our children when we don't know exactly what to say?

Some of us had to find out on our own, only we didn't have the internet. We had magazines (*Playboy*; *Hustler*), libraries with dictionaries and encyclopedias, HBO and "Skinemax" (Cinemax late night), movies (*Porky's*; *All the Right Moves*; *Fast Times at Ridgemont High*), books (*Forever*; *Are You There God? It's Me, Margaret*). Our resources were not perfect, but they served to give some information attempting to fill in the blanks when no one would talk to us. It wasn't comprehensive, that's for sure. To this, there are some parents who say, "It was good enough for me . . ." But was it really? I guess if you look at that list, there's really not much difference between then and now in terms of media sources. Except we just add the internet to the mix and that has its own issues.

Some parents assume their child knows everything there is to know about sex and sexuality already, so they hold back on talking with their child. Other parents in this same group have the added concern that their child knows some details but may not know the right facts. Both of these are legitimate concerns, knowing how much sex and sexuality is available on the internet and in other media these days—and not all of it is good or sex-positive information.

Permission

He who asks is a fool for five minutes,
but he who does not ask remains a fool forever.

~Chinese Proverb

If nothing else, this book should be one that gives you permission to talk to your children (of all ages) about the topics around human sexuality and to feel comfortable acknowledging how comfortable or uncomfortable doing so is for you. Your vulnerability about the subject is human and important for children to see, so they don't have to think they are just supposed to "know" everything as well.

I think it is time we change the typical approach to educating our children about sex and sexuality from "The Talk," a one-time conversation, to a continuous, honest, age-appropriate conversation. The Germans call it "Aufklärung," and in this context it means "to uncover the previously uncovered thing" or to enlighten; my definition of this enlightenment is sexual education that results in understanding and the spread of knowledge. I prefer the term "Aufklärung" as well because it takes the word "sex" out of the conversation, and I think that would help people move forward.

Another reason to think of these conversations about sex as being ongoing versus one time: kids can repeat commercial jingles. They do so because it is the same message over and over; consistency is the key. The same is true with talking about the messages around sex and sexuality. All of the five concepts I discuss in this book are to be learned and developed in a gradual and consistent way. When we can practice their use over and over, we will be better able to hone these skills for better relationships when we are older.

I propose something different than your typical sex education. This is not about teaching children "How to Have Sex." It's about laying the foundation to help our children develop healthy adult sexuality. The five concepts—Communication, Consent, Respect, Pleasure, and Fantasy—are complementary to either abstinence only or a comprehensive sex education. These Five Building Blocks to a Healthy Sexuality are items to help with conversations about sexuality so parents can have these chats early and often. There is not much sense in waiting until children are in school to start these important conversations. At that point, it's like trying to teach someone basic math when they already know multiplication. This book is a parenting book with a human sexuality focus, illustrated with pop culture. It gives you my suggestions for a new approach.

What Is Sexuality?

My definition of sexuality for this book is the capacity for sexual feelings, behaviors, relationships, and intimacy. Sexuality, for lots of people, is a broad yet binary thing. Others think sexuality is sexual orientation (or a person's sexual preference), but that is part of gender. But as with gender, people think in very simple yet binary terms: male or female, heterosexual or homosexual, feminine or masculine, penis or vagina. Sexuality is so much more than that. And anything but binary. Let's think about sexuality in the much broader spectrum that it really is: things like gender, relationship skills, and any of those five building blocks. It requires taking the focus and fear away from thinking of our children in sexual acts and giving us parents a different mindset to focus on less scary things—but things that absolutely will help our children develop a healthy sexuality.

I use the Five Building Blocks to a Healthy Sexuality to illustrate issues directly relating to human sexuality. When we fail to acknowledge each of the five building blocks and focus only on *penises in vaginas*, we do a disservice to being able to build a solid foundation for healthy adult sexuality. I truly believe that many of the sexual dysfunctions or issues that we have in our society today stem from the lack of learning around one or more of the five building blocks.

I have been actively raising my children using these five blocks. We openly talk as situations arise. My children tell me when enough is enough. But they also ask me questions, and I try to answer as simply and completely as I can. I also let them drive the follow-up questions, and they often take the conversation off in directions I never would have anticipated. But for them the answer to whatever question they're asking is what they seek and want to know at the moment. Personally, I know that whenever I ask a question, it's because I'm ready to know the answer. If the answer doesn't soak in for me, it's usually because I'm not ready to know.

Sex education is not a "one size fits all" prospect. This is also why there really isn't an exact age I can recommend for specific bits of information about sex. You know your own child best. Every child and adult is different. Guidelines can work, but again, it depends on the audience. The best we can do is to communicate consistently and be open and honest. The first time a baby reaches for its penis or its vulva, the recommended response is a calm, matter of fact, "Oh, you're touching your penis (or vulva)," and move on. Start at the beginning. It's natural. They are sexual (not sexy!) beings in those little cherub bodies. It's part of who they are, it's who we are, and our sexuality is not separate from who we are. And we should accept it as an integral part of them. For their entire lives, sexuality should be something we at least acknowledge. And acknowledging is different from encouraging; children don't need encouragement to go out and explore things that feel natural to them. There is no need to tell children explicitly they need to masturbate. Yet acknowledging that people do indeed masturbate can make the difference between a person developing a healthy habit versus an unhealthy obsession. This behavior feels really good, yet a person can develop such immense guilt or shame because they are told NOT to masturbate or some other damaging message. The five building blocks help us also by taking away the focus from the often scary and unnecessarily hetero-centric focus solely on what penises do in vaginas.

I hope this book teaches you how to help your children discuss their emotional and relationship needs. Sex is only one component of helping our children have successful LOVE lives. Consider this: Where do we receive the training on love and relationships? Are we modeling this for our children? If so, how? Hopefully, this book can give you food for thought in your own relationships as well as tools to support you as you help your child grow.

Dating, Love, and Sex

If you are a parent, I'm sure you get more than a little nervous thinking about your children growing up, starting to date, and falling in love. If you are like me, you probably also get nervous thinking about these children having sex one day. I know this is inevitable. I cannot stop my children from doing or experiencing anything. And really, neither can you. What you and I can do is inform ourselves, educate ourselves, so we don't deprive our children of information they need to make critical decisions of their own.

There are plenty of varying attitudes on this topic. Plenty of parents, some hetero-normative dads in particular, voice the "not on my watch" mindset. Others share a "Be good. If you can't be good, be careful. If you can't be careful, don't name it after me." philosophy. Yet most people, upon deeper discussion, recognize both of these attitudes are not helpful to their child. Children need to hear real information, a.k.a. the truth. I also think it is critical to share your own values around dating, sex, and love. More traditional thinking parents struggle with this. Let's say you are the parent/caregiver of a daughter and you think girls should not call boys. Note that this could be a source for future conflict if you take a hard line. Take a moment to evaluate your values. Why do you believe girls should not call boys? Do you believe boys and girls cannot be friends? Let's pretend she needs to call a boy classmate to get clarity on a class assignment. How will you react? Would that be okay? Will it cause a fight? How do these archaic rules work if your child is gender non-binary? Whatever your thoughts on this, share your values with your child so they understand why you feel the way you do. Own it. Is it okay for other families to approach this topic differently? Make sure you tell her that some people might do things differently, but this is what you value. A different approach doesn't make it wrong, just different.

Most parents, not surprisingly, wish to protect their children from the potential pain, shame, hurt, and embarrassment of dating and love. We all know the depiction of an over-protective father holding a shotgun, threatening any date who dares to try the sexual things he himself did when he was younger. Let's think about this model: Is this the right message? How will our children perceive it? Will they be humiliated, embarrassed? Angered by the lack of trust? Would it send fear into the suitors so they keep their hands to themselves or would it inspire them to be rebellious? Perhaps we experienced these things as young people—think back to when you and your friends were young. Chances are you or some of your classmates were already sexually active at a young age; would you freak out if your children were doing those same things? Have you started hyperventilating yet?

As an educator, I want to make sure I give my children information about sexually transmitted infections (STIs) and pregnancy prevention, but I also want to be sex-positive, which is "an attitude towards human sexuality that regards all consensual sexual activities as fundamentally healthy and pleasurable and encourages sexual pleasure and experimentation." The first part of this is what I wish to address now in this book. The second part is what we will address later—over time—naturally as our children get older and as the topic comes up. There is already enough out there that is sex-negative and scary. I don't want sex to be scary to my children because I know it can be enjoyable. Most sex education programs simply teach reproductive biology and STI/pregnancy prevention. I also want to make sure my children learn stuff related to sex and sexuality that is NOT taught in a traditional "abstinence-only before marriage" sex education program. If these are not taught in schools, then where do our children learn these important things?

In Europe, they tie sex to love, and statistics show it is a WHOLE lot more effective than the abstinence-only before marriage sex education programs here in the United States. Slate.com published a slide show with some interesting data:

> *The first time they had sex, 64 percent of Dutch teens used birth control, compared with only 26 percent of American teens. Most of the time, the Dutch teens used pills. Think about it for a minute: the majority of Dutch teens are making an appointment, going to a clinic, getting a prescription filled, and starting birth control before they have sex. Meanwhile in the United States, the average time between first having sex and first making a family-planning visit is almost two years. Here, 70 percent of school-based health clinics are forbidden from providing condoms or other birth control, even as 80 percent of them are busy diagnosing STDs and pregnancy.*[4]
>
> *In addition, almost half of the Dutch children used both condoms for STD protection and the pill or another like method for birth control. This even has a nickname: "Double Dutch!" Only 17 percent of American children protected themselves this way.*

As a parent, I want to tie sex and pleasure together. I've blogged about sex and love[5] and how there is a bit of a set up for girls to "give it up" when they think they are in love or that their partner is in love with them. Either way, there has to be talk about pleasure and love. If you keep it clinical and don't acknowledge the nuances, you are missing an incredible opportunity to connect with your child. They need to know your honest experiences so they can understand where you are coming from, and so they can avoid your mistakes as well. It's a way of imparting knowledge, which, combined with their own experiences will help them gain wisdom.

I've also blogged about dating as a single mother[6]. I am hoping my experiences are helping my daughters develop healthy views on dating and love. I am hoping to model positive behavior for them, including learning from when and if I stumble. If that happens and I can make it age-appropriate, I will sit down with them to go through a post-mortem of sorts. I've been doing this, and as a result of this open dialogue, we are strengthening the protective feelings for one another. Once not too long ago, Marcia said to me, "Mom, if he doesn't see that you are a good person, then he doesn't deserve to be with you." She was nine years old. I was absolutely blown away by that statement and have tried to encourage her to remember that for when she gets older.

I think we all have a unique perspective to offer to our children. For those of you who are married (or in a steady, committed relationship), you have a wonderful opportunity to model love, affection, compassion, and communication in relationships. I believe very strongly that children learn what they live. Let's help them live in happiness and love.

We are all trying to protect our children; that is our job as parents. Your approach may be entirely different, and that's okay. But ultimately this is about communication and providing our children with as much truthful information about dating, love, and sex as possible. For you parents of older children, consider any successes and failures you and your children experienced and learn from those when you talk to your other kids.

How Are Things Now?

What is the attitude in your house like around the topic of

sex? If you have daughters, is the image of a father with a shotgun prevalent? It is so common to joke about never letting your daughter date. That attitude comes through, and the intimidating image may set the foundation that you believe your daughter and her potential partner cannot be trusted. It also establishes a perceived prejudgment and may prevent your daughter from coming forth and talking to you. If you have sons, is your approach to all things relational or sexual (masturbation, making out, dating)? The message that you communicate nonverbally in this approach is that the feelings and emotions about what they are experiencing are things that should not be shared or even talked about. Upon closer examination, both of these examples can be a set up for potential failure later in life.

Every Family Is Different and Every Region Has Its Own Influence

I have a few friends who were raised to believe sex was not bad or scary. There was no fear or anxiety around sex, and as a result, these people can more easily communicate openly with their partners about their own sexual and nonsexual needs, wants, and desires, including fantasy. In turn, they are equipped with the skills to listen to and accept the same from their partners. I grew up in a fairly standard Midwestern household, one that was very sexually repressed, and my parents were hesitant to talk to me about this topic. I wish the conversations could have been easier with my parents but now as an adult, I understand why they refused. This topic is intimidating!

Early in my blogging career, a friend wrote to me about my nontraditional subject matter: "Most of the people between NYC and Malibu are rather prudish by the coast's standards. I'd soften [your message] a bit so Middle America can be more accepting of the message . . . ." Perhaps it's more of a difference between metropolitan, suburban, and rural areas but generally, I don't think Middle America is so different really.

I have talked to hundreds of people about their conversations with their children from people local to me here in the Bay Area to people from across the country. One friend in the Midwest shared with me that he has talked to his children openly about sex from a very early age, and his nearly twenty-year-old daughter at one point considered becoming a nun. I think this was a fantastic example of a young person educated in sexuality who knows herself and felt empowered to choose her own path.

An OB/GYN friend of mine in California and I had a conversation about talking to children openly about sex. She has two daughters of her own, high school and college aged. The high schooler used to describe to her parents the behaviors she observed at the teen parties: Lipstick Parties, a.k.a. parties where the teen girls would perform oral sex on the boys, leaving a lipstick ring on the penis (which was shocking really, considering the teens received the usual abstinence-only/reproductive-biology-as-sex-ed in high school, but that's not my point here). Both of her daughters decided to wait until later for their sexual experiences. How much later? Both were older than the US average for age at first intercourse, which is seventeen[7]. The teens described above received information that didn't make them overly curious to go out and explore what the big secret about sex was.

Few of us got any information, let alone good information about sex. Looking at the bright side of this upbringing and given my interest in sexual practices and behavior, I sought out the information—open, honest, and accurate information—and now I am dedicating my life to trying to help you and other families have an open, truly communicative household where children can talk to their parents about these very important things.

Teens Will Be Teens

Teens are going to do what they are going to do mainly because they don't see the reasons not to engage sexually the same way adults do. For teens, becoming sexually active can be about popularity, acceptance, or belonging, among other things. Rarely are the things adults consider deterrents taken into consideration: STIs, pregnancy, emotional disappointment, etc. This is understandable if you know a little about adolescent brain development. The frontal cortexes of their adolescent brains are not fully developed until almost their mid-twenties[8], so teens and young adults may not be able to see the potential consequences and risks that we adults know and recognize. Some teens think, "Those bad things won't happen to me, they happen to someone else." Was that the way YOU thought as a teen or young adult? Why should teens now be any different?

The Opposite of Permission: Verboten

In 2012, the governor of the state of Tennessee signed into law a bill that prohibits teachers from talking about so-called "Gateway Sexual Activities," such as kissing, hand-holding, and genital touching when teaching sex education in Tennessee schools[9].

According to state Rep. John DeBerry, (D-TN), in his testimony to the Tennessee House of Representatives, "Everybody in this room knows what gateway sexual activity is. Everybody knows there are certain buttons when you push them, certain switches when you turn them on, there's no stopping, especially for undisciplined, untrained, untaught, and unraised children who just want to feel affection from somebody or anybody." I have many issues with his uninformed—or at best misinformed—statement.

1. "there's no stopping."

Wrong. I believe this feeds a culture of humiliation and disrespect (a.k.a. rape culture), in addition to the misconception that people cannot control themselves once they find themselves in a turned-on situation. I disagree completely. We all CAN stop. Everyone can and should be able to think about what they are doing AND how they feel about it. To do or think otherwise is ridiculous. One can't even call it animalistic because it isn't. "The animal world is full of species that have sex only during widely spaced intervals when the female is ovulating . . . an excessively horny monkey is acting 'human,' while a man or woman uninterested in sex more than once or twice a year would be, strictly speaking, 'acting like an animal.'[10] Therefore, people who engage in sex whenever, wherever, without stopping aren't animals, they're human.

We need to teach about permission. We need to teach about boundaries (and that we all have them) and how to give and obtain consent from our friends and others.

2. "especially for the undisciplined, untrained, untaught . . ."

Um, Mr. DeBerry, that's completely the fault of the "abstinence-only before marriage" approach. How are children disciplined, trained, or taught if no one in the education system in the state of Tennessee can talk about these things? We need to teach about feelings, emotions, and how to communicate the same to others. We need to teach about respect for self and others. We need to teach about SO many things. You can't forbid educating children and then complain they are uneducated.

3. "just want to feel affection from somebody."

We all want to be loved. We all want to be accepted. Lots of people like to be held close. Yet we live in a society that sexualizes most forms of touch. I fear we are developing a touch-deprived generation. Lots of teachers, especially male ones, at the elementary school level express concern about hugging their pupils for fear of being accused of inappropriate touch. This is so sad because a few bad apples shouldn't spoil the whole bunch. Not every teacher's hug of a student is a "gateway sexual activity"—or are these the "certain buttons when you push them, certain switches when you turn them on" Mr. DeBerry is talking about? <sarcasm>. We do need to teach about pleasure and the healing power of touch—and that it's not just sexual pleasure.

These are exactly the reasons Mr. DeBerry gives that are the justification for accurate, open, and honest comprehensive sexual education. I'm just not sure why he and other "abstinence-only" proponents don't see that.

Misconceptions

My biggest pet peeve for what we teach children is this: Why do we teach girls how to prevent themselves from being abused or raped? Why do we tell them to cover themselves up? Why do we tell children to be scared of or to avoid strangers when the reality is that's not the true threat? Everyone—children, teens, and adults—needs to be taught to learn and show respect for others, and by extension, *not* to rape. This is not just for kids, though. Adults who did not grow up with education about respect for self and others—vital information, learning, and practice—need to learn or relearn and understand this as well. "Stranger Danger" (as we call it in the United States) is the idea that most unwanted sexual advances toward others come from strangers, but thanks to statistics from the Department of Justice, we know that most unwanted sexual advances come from friends and relatives. Some frightening statistics: 93 percent of juvenile sexual assault victims knew their attacker; 34 percent were family members and 59 percent were acquaintances. Only 7 percent of the perpetrators were strangers to the victim[11]. The way it is now, our messages in talking about this topic are all backwards, and it's not suiting any of us in a healthy or productive manner.

Why Is This Important?

When considering the various topics to be covered in sexuality education, the American Academy of Pediatrics[12] recommends that pediatricians encourage parents to cover the following: names of body parts, masturbation, puberty, menstruation, sexual orientation, preventing pregnancy, how to avoid STIs (sexually transmitted infections), how to protect yourself from sexual abuse, taking opportunities to initiate discussions about sexuality, (i.e., the birth of a sibling or pet), encouraging parents to answer their children's questions accurately, and promoting communication and safety within social relationships. Even the American Academy of Pediatrics says pediatricians should "acknowledge that sexual activity may be pleasurable but also must be engaged in responsibly." These are only a few. Many of these are covered in this book.

I'm personally not a big fan of leaving these important conversations to anyone else alone. The results can be even better when the information comes from many good sources, but I believe parents are the best source for morals, personal motivations, and ethics about sex and sexuality.

Many parents have a difficult time discussing sexuality with their children. It's understandable. Not many of us received a good sex education when we were growing up. I think if parents step back from their assumptions and realize that the conversations that lead up to the tougher questions about sex and sexuality can be so basic. This stuff doesn't have to be scary; the concepts that need to be discussed before talking about the more advanced stuff are so elementary. It is a lot like math; you don't start with calculus. Teachers typically start with more basic concepts before building on the knowledge base. The things we will talk about in this book are concepts in preparation for later puberty education classes in school. This is what I propose in this book.

This is not about encouraging pedophilia—far from it. I am not encouraging, endorsing, or suggesting adults sexually engage with children. That is not where I am going with this. With as many as one in four women and one in six men experiencing sexual violence in their lifetime, it's clear we need to revamp how we talk about sex completely[13]. Make no mistake, the information adults should share is for the child to process and absorb, to learn to make good decisions on their own.

We should keep in mind how important it is to teach what healthy relationships look like. There are lots of things to learn and consider before partnering up; have you considered how you learned what you needed to learn as it relates to relationships and love? I don't recall having a course on that in school. Most of my learning about love and relationships was through watching the people around me, gleaning information from the things that were (and were not) said and listening to my gut about what felt good and what did not. This was not a perfect process; a little guidance from informed, trusted sources would have been great. Children want to hear from their parents about sexuality; they are assumed to be a trusted source.

Let's use that trust responsibly.

I've been covering the topic of teaching parents and their children about sexuality for almost six years now. One of the questions I get is why I do this work. Here's why: I remember what it was like to grow up as a girl in the United States. I remember being uncomfortable in my own skin. I remember being secretly curious about the *Playboy* magazines I would find. I remember being uncomfortably shy about my body, which in many ways was just the nakedness. I remember being grossed out by porn. I remember not knowing how to ask for what I wanted sexually. I remember faking orgasms (why did I do that?). I grew up in a pretty typical American household where no one talked about sex. But it was everywhere around me in movies and books, and I didn't know why adults had a weird attitude about all of it. There was no *Joy of Sex* on any bookshelf in my childhood home. I was confused, uncertain, insecure, and felt guilty about my interests and desires. What I want for my children is for them to be secure, confident, comfortable in their own skin, unashamed, kind to others, but also strong in who they are—not allowing someone else to push them around. I want them to grow up without the same sort of anxiety I had about sex because, while it's a vitally important part of life, there really isn't that much to be scared of when it comes to who we are and who we can be.

One of my areas of focus as a sexologist and sex educator is helping parents—and other adults who care for children—to shift their thinking about sex education for the next generation. I see the education of our youth in sexuality as a process of enlightenment: sex education that results in understanding and the spread of knowledge.

A Quick Note About Language

I use the term **parent** with the intention to be inclusive of all adults who are caregivers to the children in their charge. This includes teachers, aunts, uncles, grandparents, foster and adoptive parents, etc. Whether someone has a blood relation to a child or not doesn't diminish in any way their ability to care for and advise a child on such matters. I am, of course, assuming the best intentions on your part as the adult to be responsible and "do no harm" to the child's emotional, physical, or psychological well-being.

Of course, not all children have parents who have the time to cover such topics, have parents who aren't operating with the best interest of the child in mind, or have no parents at all. These children deserve good information as well, and their caregivers can do so with good resources and support.

I also need to highlight the **inclusivity of sexualities other than heterosexual and gender as a spectrum.** While I have not emphasized this in my wording throughout, as a professional sexologist I want you to know that even if you do not believe homosexuality or sexual orientations other than heterosexuality exist in real life, they do indeed. The same with people who identify as transgender or intersex. And you will encounter this everywhere you go. Certainly, everywhere people can freely express themselves without fear of bodily harm and abuse. Consider this: How do our messages about sex and sexuality affect children and young adults who identify as anything other than typical, straight, male, or female? Please consider the huge step forward for humanity if everyone stopped fighting this simple fact. Given that, I also want to point out that regardless of a child's gender identity, gender expression, or sex assigned at birth, you can still use the concepts in this book as well as the Five Building Blocks to a Healthy Sexuality to talk about sexuality. Everyone deserves to have accurate information about this topic. I certainly hope you would love and adore your child regardless of their sexual orientation or gender identification. Please consider extending this consideration to anyone else as well. For those who identify as more scripturally aligned, "love one another" is one thing I was taught when I was growing up. Search for that in your hearts; I hope it's still out there.

Speaking of which, it is my goal to encourage us to create a **culture of active (and enthusiastic) consent** where sex is a positive experience. I think many of you out there wish for happy, positive, and dare I say, pleasurable experiences for your children once they grow up; **ideally their first sexual experiences will be with partners of their own conscious choice in the timeframe that they are most comfortable with.** The way things are right now is not working. Kids don't get good information or people won't talk about it, so they go off to "figure it out on their own." Or they use alcohol or other substances that cloud their judgment and find themselves in a time or place when they might make a different choice if they were sober. Or someone else makes a choice for them—whether through coercion or rape—that they will become sexual. I think we can all agree that none of those scenarios are ideal. Yet keeping this topic in the dark is failing us all. Our children deserve better than to carry our guilt and shame with them as well; it's not their baggage to carry. This is possible, but we do have to spend some time working on ourselves simultaneously. I believe we can do this.

The Five Building Blocks to a Healthy Sexuality

Nothing is particularly hard if you divide it into small jobs.

~Henry Ford

In the United States, when one talks about sex education to parents, many people cringe. Some people think of sex education as teaching children different sexual positions. On the contrary, it is my opinion that we need to expand our thinking beyond merely thinking of sex as intercourse and break things down into even more basic terms.

The foundation for my approach to sex education is The Five Building Blocks to a Healthy Sexuality. I believe each of these blocks is a core component that needs to be discussed as we teach young people about sex and sexuality, regardless of whether an "abstinence-only before marriage" or comprehensive sex education approach is used. The five blocks are, from the bottom up: Communication, Consent, Respect, Pleasure, and Fantasy. Because they're building blocks, you need to begin at the bottom if you want to build a stable foundation.

I will discuss these five more completely next, and you will see practical examples and anecdotes. I discovered these five as a result of my training at the Institute for Advanced Study of Human Sexuality and from being a mother. Through my readings and sitting through lectures, I learned about the many different and varied issues, problems, and concerns that people have around sex. As someone who gets enjoyment out of finding patterns, some emerged in my studies. The five building blocks are those patterns. When I learned about rape, I saw it as a failure to teach about some very basic concepts, none of which I was seeing taught in human sexuality courses which seemed only to focus on anatomy and physiology (often without inclusion of the clitoris), reproductive biology, and STI/pregnancy prevention. Every other issue or problem seemed to be a failure to teach about one of or some combination of the building blocks. Being a problem-solver and a mother, I naturally sought out to fix this thing I saw was broken for my children's benefit and for the benefit of others. These five blocks are a step in the right direction.

In my approach, the most important lessons about sex are not even about the "how-to." Instead, it's about Communication, Consent, Respect, Pleasure, and Fantasy. The majority of my work is a version of "continuing education" or "train the trainer" lessons for adults. I want to help adults to get the tools, knowledge, and comfort to talk about sex with their children and other young people with whom they have contact, openly and honestly.

Whittling down to these five concepts came from years of studying about human sexual behavior, learning about dysfunction in all types, and hearing personal stories of struggle around the topics of human sexuality. These blocks are important, whether a person is two or

102 years old. These concepts can be learned and applied at any age.

"Sex." What's the first thing that comes to mind?

Much of the shame and guilt we have in our attitudes about sex, including our fears, has much to do with the emotions that we sensed and the feelings we experienced and picked up on from the adults in our lives when we were growing up. Children typically don't question the messages they get from adults. Once children become adults, they are then at risk of passing these complicated and unresolved emotions on to their children. If we don't address the subtle indoctrination that takes place, then our unhealthy attitudes never change. This book, I hope, is the beginning of that change for the better.

When I talk about sexual topics and the importance of talking to children about them, there is a very clear distinction between "acknowledging" and "encouraging" the sexuality of children; I don't think we need to encourage sexuality at all. Children are going to do what they're going to do whether we like it or not. It's a matter of us as adults to listen, be empathetic, and understand that we are all sexual beings.

Some people say that discussing the topics of sex and sexuality with children "takes away their innocence," but I disagree with that. Children already have minds that are more open than our adult minds. Lots of adults make almost anything into a sexual joke. Children, on the other hand, just don't think like that . . . at least not until you teach them to. And oh yes, do we teach them. We do so in the things that we snicker about, thinking children don't understand what we're talking about; they may not get the exact joke, but they'll learn that it's hush-hush topic. We encourage it in the TV shows and the movies they see that contain the subtle adult jokes we think children don't see or hear, they do. Children understand more than we think they do. Children pick up on the nuance probably more adeptly than adults do. So, innocence is "lost" the moment we lie to them through the sin of omission. Whoever knows the right thing to do and fails to do it is the one causing problems. Children trust us to guide them. It's not worth it to break that trust just because we think we know better.

We do more harm to our children by keeping them in the dark. We potentially do our children harm when we don't allow them to know the proper terms of their bodies. We potentially do our children harm when we fail to acknowledge the ways to teach them that extend beyond the "penis in vagina" way of thinking about sex. We potentially do our children harm when we make girls the gatekeepers of sexuality and establish boys as wild and untamable subjects to their urges. We potentially do our children harm when we don't teach our children that others deserve our respect just as much as we deserve respect. We can do better for our children.

I encourage you to read this book with an open mind. For many of you, the way I talk about things will challenge the ways you may have been brought up to think. Permit yourself to question why sex was presented to you in the way it was and how a different approach may have benefitted you and could indeed benefit your children. I also want to encourage you to ask yourself questions. If you find yourself getting upset as you read this book, why? If you find yourself getting angry at the things I propose, why? Does it have anything to do with the attitudes of the adults around you when you were growing up? Does it have anything to do with a personal experience? I want to encourage you to examine your feelings as they come up as you read this book. I want you to notice if there's something that really bothers you, why? How far back can you go to find the root cause?

Hey, I don't profess to be perfect in any way. I'm probably going to freak some of you out by the conversations that we have. I'll probably frustrate others that I'm saying anything about the topic. I do believe, however, that if I give my own children all of the information they need about sex and the associated feelings (most importantly, feelings!) that they will then in time make good, healthy decisions about what they choose to do, with whom, and when. I think the same is true for all children. There are those who believe boys should be the "safeguards" of sexuality and girls should cherish fidelity. I think there is long-term value in acknowledging that girls can and should expect pleasure out of their sexual interactions just as there is long-term value in acknowledging that both boys AND girls should earn respect for each other to share that pleasure.

As I've said, I'm personally not a big fan of leaving these important conversations about sex and sexuality to anyone else alone. I'm sure you don't want that either. Learning can be even better when the information comes from many good sources, but I firmly believe parents are the BEST first source for morals, personal motivations, and ethics about sex and sexuality. All the other resources available to you are there for you to learn and grow as well. This book, I hope, will be part of a beginning of personal growth for you and maybe even growth in your relationships with your partner and/or your children.

All adults can be empowered and enlightened sexually to be able to make solid decisions for themselves, to know how to protect themselves, and to decide when, where, and how they want to be sexual. These decisions are no different for a child. This book will hopefully give you more freedom and comfort to communicate with your child, and in turn, give your child the confidence they need to make the best informed decisions in life and develop healthy adult sexuality.

Each of the following five chapters will begin with my working definition of the building block as a concept. Then I provide a little more detail about some of the key components. The blogs at the end of each chapter feature a few examples of how I have applied the teachings personally. The text provides the information (and hopefully some motivation as well), and the blogs give behavioral examples. I have already explained how I began to identify the Five Building Blocks to a Healthy Sexuality. Later I will share how I began to see some of the problems that arise in our culture as a failure to teach about any one or a combination of the five blocks. But before I skip ahead, here's a visual reminder of the blocks and how they build on each other (and they

The Five Building Blocks to a Healthy Sexuality

Communication

If we can only make it clear that feelings are mentionable and manageable, we will have done a great service for mental health.

~ Fred Rogers, in his speech to the US Senate in 1969

Communication: *Being able to communicate feelings and emotions, understanding that emotion is not a bad thing, communicating needs, wants, desires and listening to the same in others, tuning in to the body language of others. Communication through touch, encouraging and modeling communication (in general), and using the correct terminology.*

This is the most elementary yet critical item of the five building blocks, which is why it's where to start. I believe many of the problems, issues, and challenges we have as adults in our own interpersonal relationships have to do with this block in particular. And many of these issues can be helped when learned at a young age. We can start by breaking them down into these smaller, bite-sized components and how they relate to raising children to be sexually healthy adults.

Recognize, Identify, and Communicate Feelings and Emotions

Being able to recognize, identify, and most importantly, communicate what one is feeling is important for children, as well as adults. It requires adults to get in tune with this first, though, so we can effectively help our children.

The challenge is that many people find ways to numb themselves from feeling any emotions. At some point, many people stop listening to their bodies, which some people call "listening to their gut." The question is how does this happen? Sometimes it happens quickly, sometimes it takes years. Sometimes this split happens while one is still growing up. It can start with having your intuition stunted, being told that what you're feeling is wrong, or not being able to exercise your boundaries (which ties to the next section about consent). As a person gets older, the split could occur because of drugs or alcohol or submerging oneself in an activity like work, gambling, shopping, etc. Some parents even numb themselves by doing everything for their kids or others and nothing for themselves.

The second question is why does this happen? For lots of reasons, like stress, pain, and broken hearts. It's easier to escape into something else when it distracts one from bigger issues. Not permitting oneself to feel the highs and lows of life's emotional roller coaster is a form of emotional procrastination; at some point, it's going to come out and likely not in good ways. Also, a person cannot selectively numb their self; if you numb one emotion, you numb them all.

In an interview with Yahoo.com Health, Julianna Deardorff, PhD, author of *The New Puberty*, said parents could help their daughters through puberty by "providing consistency, by managing their own emotions when daughters are struggling with theirs, and by teaching their daughters to regulate and express their feelings appropriately during this time of rapid change."[14] This consistency helps all kids.

Modeling the behavior we want to see is important as well. Now I know, no one is perfect. Lots of parents snap at their children when it's not their fault. When that happens, it is okay to circle back, apologize, and admit to your children that it wasn't okay for you to lose your cool. If it's appropriate, you can share what the cause was so they understand it wasn't them. Of course, there are times when snapping is a result of them not doing what you asked. In that instance, I have found when I shared that I was frustrated because I needed to ask multiple times and requested that they empty the dishwasher, they responded. I notice that in that instance it's my conscious direction that they complete that chore that gets results . . . certainly, my snapping didn't. All of this requires parents also to have a level of awareness where they recognize and identify their own feelings to be able to stay in tune for the benefit of their child. Puberty is rough—so much is happening to those growing bodies and brains that it can be really confusing without information or context or guidance.

Modeling vulnerability as a parent is also very important. Children look up to their parents. We all want to appear perfect and impenetrable, but it does not hurt for them to see that you are real and imperfect because it permits them to be the same.

So why are feelings and emotions such an important part of communication? How many of us have been in the presence of someone who was mentally or emotionally checked out? How does that feel? This sort of distance doesn't allow for a good connection between people. As I'm writing this, I hear myself begin to sound a bit esoteric or "woo woo." But taking that risk, I'll go even further to say that this connection between people is what makes sex between adults, as adults, feel even more amazing. As people get older, they begin to discover "The Keys to Good Sex:" education, communication, and exploration.

Know Emotion Is Not a Bad Thing for Children

Our society would benefit from every individual understanding that having and expressing emotions is a good thing. We need to be aware of how we handle children sharing their feelings. Older generations have a different way of handling this, and some are really crummy ways that hurt children emotionally. When I was away lecturing in China for two weeks, my mother was staying with my children. My nine-year-old was missing me. She would cry and cry. My mother told her not to cry because it made other people feel bad. Not the right thing to say. I would have cleared that up for my child right then by explaining to her that:

1. It is not her responsibility to make anyone else happy.
2. She has permission to feel sad or whatever feeling it is.
3. I encourage her to acknowledge her feelings (lonely, sad, etc.) and to figure out things she can do that make herself feel better.

Then we discussed things that would work for her. Other toxic versions that embed this emotional stoicism in our children are, "I'll give you something to cry about" and "children should be seen and not heard." These lazy responses to our children expressing feelings are really messed up. They will shut children down and they will cease to share important emotions.

Denying our emotions can be bad for us. If you're a believer that the mind can somaticize issues into problems, then check out Louise Hay's[15] book *Heal Your Body* about metaphysical causations. Our bodies are amazing, and they tell us when something's wrong.

Telling boys [and girls] to "man up" is detrimental to everyone. Men can and should be permitted to have and express feelings. Expressing feelings is not just something women are supposed to do, and there is nothing wrong with women who do. It takes men years to undo the damage that has been done in their formative years. The organization The Representation Project has done great work with raising awareness of the damage the phrase "be a man" has had on boys and men. Check out their documentary, *The Mask You Live In*[16]. There is nothing wrong with giving a child a hug when they are in pain (I'll talk about this again in the pleasure section). Ted Zeff, in his 2013 book *Raise an Emotionally Healthy Boy*,[17] advises, "Show vulnerability with your son, rather than being someone who has all the answers and always has to be right. Your boy will learn humility when you apologize to him when you make a mistake" and "Give your young son frequent hugs and kisses. A dad who can show affection to his son is modeling love and compassion." Wonderful, sound advice. Hugging a child and/or allowing them to witness an "undesired" emotion does great things for them. Trust me, teaching and modeling compassion to children is not a bad thing. Children look for love, care, and concern from the adults in their life. Support and compassion go a long way.

Communicate Needs, Wants, Desires, and Listen to the Same

It is important to teach children that it is okay to communicate our needs, wants, and desires (NWD) and listen to the same from others. Communicating this is part of the type of practice we need as children so that we can communicate effectively when we grow up and start practicing in our relationships with others. Listening to your partner without judgment is important as well. Each of us has our NWD but so do our partners; in relationships this stuff is a two-way street. Some people don't tend to share their NWD if they sense that they are going to be judged—others don't share because they are concerned about hurting their partner's feelings. Some of this holding back comes from people believing emotion is a bad thing; the spoken or unspoken messages we received as children dictate how we handle this sharing and/or being judged. Our NWD is important, and just like our voices, they deserve to be heard.

Mister Rogers' Neighborhood on PBS was a television show for children when I was growing up. In 1969, the US Senate held a hearing to determine funding for the fledgling network. Mr. Rogers gave a speech to the US Senate[18] panel and discussed his television show and how his work was for the benefit of children. In his testimony, he said, "If we can only make it clear that feelings are mentionable and manageable it would be a great service to mental health." This is so true, and I'd like to take it a step further and say this is important for our sexual health. Why? Fast forward to adulthood. Feelings allow one to connect with another person. If you have been unable to express your feelings as a child or young adult, it may be difficult to do so as an adult. Feelings are important and everyone has them, but some are not as easily able to express. The people who talk about having the best sex of their life[19] usually are talking about communication and consent.

One of my favorite sexual moments was in a conversation with a partner about whether or not we would or should have sex. There's a happy feeling knowing you're with a partner who is listening to youone of trust and security. And afterward, I had an overwhelming feeling of being satisfied and satiated. Imagine if this is how it always is for all of us!

Tuning into Body Language: Communication through Touch

In 2013, I went to my first Cuddle Party[20]. The concept of Cuddle Party was created in 2004 by Reid Mihalko and Marcia Baczynski as a way for adults to learn communication, boundaries, and affection. In a nonsexual setting, you can meet new people, practice asking for what you want and saying "no" to what you don't want in a safe space structured for exploration and enjoyment. To practice rejecting others, being rejected, and learning that it's not the end of the world is vitally important. A Cuddle Party is also a fantastic way to learn and reinforce the concept that not all touch is sexual touch; a massage can absolutely be just that and doesn't have to lead to sexual behavior, which is a wonderful thing to learn. At a Cuddle Party, one also learns about consent, touch, and negotiation. I will talk about consent more in the next chapter.

Communication is more than just words—we should listen to our gut. We should notice and pay attention to—even ask about—body language. Check in and make sure other people are okay. It is also good to pay attention to people's actions and ask when there is a discrepancy. Sometimes people "say" things with their bodies that are different from the words coming out of their mouths. There is a reason people say, "Actions speak louder than words." What they say doesn't always match up. Also, tune into your own body language—are you uncomfortable, shy, or otherwise closed off? Matching your unspoken body language to your emotions is an important lesson for people of all ages.

Encouraging and Modeling Communication

It is important to encourage your children to communicate with you. If a child does something we wouldn't do or that might put them at risk of harm—like flash someone online—they must know they are not alone if they should ever find themselves in trouble. A situation like this happened in 2012; *The New Yorker* ran a story about a young Canadian teen named "Amanda Todd."[21]

She was chatting with someone she met online, a man who flattered her. At his request, she flashed him. The man took a picture of her breasts. He then proceeded to follow Todd around the internet for years. He asked her to put on another show for him, but she refused. So, he'd find her classmates on Facebook and send them the photograph. To cope with the anxiety, Todd descended into drugs and alcohol, ill-advised flirtations, and sex. Her classmates ostracized her. She attempted suicide a few times before finally succeeding.

Just like adults, children need a trusted adult they can go to in such instances. Together, you and your child can go to the authorities. Perhaps they can go after the person threatening and blackmailing the child. A united front can work to stop the online harassment and make your child feel empowered because they have your support. Many times, it is an innocent enough mistake that spirals into something a lot worse.

Similarly, it's important to be aware of the messages you share even when they're not directed at your child. Things a child overhears you say to others can be messages that are internalized. Think about what people say when they are gossiping; let's say you hear about a young teen becoming pregnant out of wedlock, like Bristol Palin. I've heard parents say within earshot of their child, "I would disown her if that happened to my daughter!" It might be posturing or playing to be morally superior with the person in your conversation, but in either case it doesn't instill the trust or security children would need from the adults in their life should they find themselves in such a challenging situation.

Correct Terminology

There are many reasons why parents should teach children the correct medical terms and encourage their use. I see absolutely no downside to using the proper anatomical terms with your child when talking with them about their genitals. If saying the terms is tough for you, then consider the challenge yours. You will have to confront your own shame, guilt, or embarrassment head on with regards to not being able to say the words. Trust me, once you can say "vulva" in mixed company and don't break a sweat or descend into giggles, then you have gotten past the stage most third or fourth graders are in. After that point, it's easy. This is also why you should start using the medical names for body parts when children are infants and toddlers; it's like exercising muscle memory. Get used to it while they're young, it won't be a big deal for you to say it when they're older. Kids will try to push your buttons or embarrass you. Especially if you are squeamish. I know people who did this to their parents. At a museum your child might say in a loud voice, "Look mama! That statue has boobs!" either to embarrass you publicly or just because of the novelty. If you react like it is not a big deal, ("Yes, dear. They're called breasts."), they will get bored with the game. You will notice that after the novelty of shocking you wears off, the "bad" words won't have the same power they used to have. Then saying "penis" or "clitoris" in front of you in the store is no longer "fun" for them. I have taken my children aside later and explained to them that certain words are not polite to say in the company of certain people and one should refrain from saying them out of respect (another building block we will discuss later) for others such as grandparents or others who may not talk that way.

Parents should start with naming the parts of the body using the anatomically correct terms. Using the correct terms with children promotes positive body image, self-confidence, and parent-child communication. It also discourages perpetrators and, in the event of abuse, helps children and adults navigate the disclosure and forensic interview process,[22] according to Laura Palumbo, a prevention specialist with the National Sexual Violence Resource Center (NSVRC). Would you ever tell your daughter her nose was called something else? Would you tell your child his ear was called some different or goofy word? Why would you treat the genitals any differently? I know saying these words out loud to a lover, let alone to anyone else, can be a source of embarrassment if you let it. Children, especially tweens and teens, know what's embarrassing to you, and if you hide the words or say them secretively instead of as matter of fact, chances are good that your child will likely milk that to their advantage. However, if you are honest, saying something along the lines of "I didn't have anyone to talk to me about this stuff (and I wish I had), so it's a little uncomfortable for me to talk about this with you but I think it's important that you get information I didn't," chances are they'll respect that honesty. Other kids might still push your buttons; they're kids. But yours will likely stop now that they know nothing entertaining will happen.

Using the proper terms also has an impact on body image. Doing so promotes the concept that the human body is natural and beautiful (which it is), whereas using euphemisms to mask shame or embarrassment perpetuates the idea that genitals are shameful. Another drawback to perpetuating this shame is the negative self-perception of our physical bodies. It's amazing how the inability to use the words translates into not being able to accept the body parts as well. I have heard of women who will not wash their external genitalia because they cannot bring themselves to touch their own vulva. Can you imagine not washing under your arms or some other part of your body because other people told you they thought it was inappropriate?

The only images we get of genitals might be from adult video or skin magazines, and those are likely photoshopped images. Some women choose to go under the knife for plastic surgery on their labia, sometimes after a lover or partner has made a disparaging comment about their labia. An Australian TV show, *Hungry Beast*[23] took a look at one of the possible reasons for labiaplasty: censorship. Since most people can't examine other people's genitals, they don't have an idea of "normal" except for what they see in adult literature such as *Playboy* or *Hustler*. Without a "real" frame of reference, it's hard to compare oneself to this odd standard. There are a few recently published books on the market that give a sense of the "real" range of what vulvas look like.[24] Taking time to look at those books and warm up to them makes them less intimidating in the long run. Seeing real bodies in images or in real life and in a non-sexualized context has a positive effect of making people less nervous about the way they look.

I encourage parents to support and honor their children as they explore and express the boundaries of their own bodies. If they don't want to hug or kiss someone, tell them okay if they're ready later they can do so then. Those are also the first steps in teaching about consent. Why is this so important? Take this example: How would a child understand the difference between their parent pushing (coercing) them to hug a friend or relative they barely know with the same friend or relative later coercing them to do something else they are uncomfortable with when mom and dad aren't around? There's no difference in my mind (and I presume in the child's mind either). The child's decision as to how they can honor their own body (keeping a safe distance until they can gauge safety for themselves) has been blurred by the trusted adult's direction (coercion) in the first instance. It is acceptable, and not disrespectful, to simply allow a child to acknowledge an unknown adult without physical contact. When you consider that 34 percent of offenders who sexually abuse children[25] are family members, it makes the boundary issues even more important.

Using the proper terminology is also helpful in preventing and, heaven forbid, dealing with occurrences of "unwanted sexual contact," also known as "child sexual abuse") with children. If one finds their own family in a situation of suspected unwanted sexual contact, I hope the child is equipped with the correct anatomical terms to use to describe where exactly on their body it happened and how it felt. I also hope that adults can listen without too much fear, pain, anxiety, judgment, or ignorance. I add ignorance here because the response or arousal that can naturally occur sometimes ends up being confusing for children who don't have the language to describe what is happening to them. It's a form of mislabeling to call it "abuse" if or when it doesn't hurt the child physically. Some feel pleasure simply because of an automatic physical response, and then they feel guilt or shame because there is a disparity between what they felt and what others tell them they should feel. Janet Rosenzweig writes in *The Sex-Wise Parent*, "We can neutralize one of the most powerful tools used by predators when we raise kids who truly understand that genital arousal in response to stimulation is as uncontrollable as getting goose bumps when they are tickled."[26] Changing the ignorance around the phrase "sexual abuse" to a more accurate description of "unwanted sexual contact" makes the child or person in this situation feel more empowered than the "victim."

So how does all of this apply in real life? One can read all theoretical advice about this topic, but what does it look like in practice? You have read my abstract thoughts and ideas. Now you can read how I have applied this knowledge in teaching my own children about human sexuality. The following blogs are just a few examples related to communication as a foundational building block.

Talk to Your Kids

My children get confused a bit when they hear stories about adults not being able to tolerate talking about sex. They just don't understand what the big deal is. Not long ago, I was reading an article about sex. Marcia was looking over my shoulder and asked what the article was about. The specific article wasn't important, so I told her that generally some people would prefer to shield their children from sex and sexual images because they think it's inappropriate for them to know and instead tell their children made up things like a stork brings a newborn baby. She asked me why they would do that. I told her even though sex is a natural part of being human, there are lots of people who are uncomfortable talking about it, and they think if you talk about it with children then the children will want to go out and do it. And as a result, it has an impact on the ability of some people to give accurate information when they talk to their children about sex.

To give Marcia another example of a child getting incorrect information, I told her about an episode of the TV show *Mad Men* where Don Draper's grade-school-aged daughter Sally said she knows what sex is and that the adult in the conversation didn't correct the misinformation because the topic was uncomfortable. Here is the dialog from the episode, "The Chrysanthemum and The Sword,"[27] between Sally Draper and her babysitter:

SD: "Are you and Daddy doing it?"

The babysitter (shocked): "What?!"

SD (boldly): "I know what 'it' is. I know that the man pees inside the woman."

Babysitter (concerned): "Where did you hear that?"

SD: "A girl at school."

Babysitter: "You should talk to your mommy."

SD (sadly): "I don't want to."

After I told Marcia this story, she said to me, "That's what kids at school say! They say that the man pees inside the woman when they have sex!" Marcia was in third grade at the time she heard this; two whole grades before this topic is even addressed in the curriculum at her school. At this young, prepubescent age, urine is the only thing that comes out of the penis, so it is understandable that children think that. Understandable, but not excusable. I was surprised at this outburst of new information and clarified it to make sure she knew that's not what happens.

I know *Mad Men* is a fictional TV show set in the 1960s. I understand this is accurate for how sex and sexuality was approached back then, but it makes me sad to think that almost fifty years later there are still many parents who are not more engaging and forthcoming than this make-believe interaction.

The conversation in this TV show very well could be a conversation in real life today. Here is a little girl who is bold enough to say she understands more than she is being told and wants to talk about it. Asking a question about the source of this "information" instead of correcting the misinformation makes it seem as if the information is correct. As I said before, not correcting misinformation is in itself a message. And when we ask where they heard the question instead of addressing the point on the table, we give the impression that the source of the information matters.

It is not necessarily the babysitter's job to discuss sex with the child—it could have been an aunt, a cousin, or another adult—but in any case, it most definitely would be up to the caregiving adult to tell the parent(s). Giving a play-by-play might be embarrassing, but the parent absolutely needs to hear what the child is asking so things can be discussed, and this is not the time to berate or belittle your child for asking. It is in this moment when the child starts asking that a parent should be open and ready to answer questions or at least be comfortable with saying, "I don't know, but let's find out together."

Something to note here: do not be angry, offended, hurt, or show any other negative emotion if your child starts the conversation about sex with someone other than you. It doesn't necessarily mean they don't trust you or feel comfortable talking to you. Perhaps the timing or situation wasn't just right to ask but take the opportunity now yourself to sit down together. When you do, please make sure you try to find a basic, matter-of-fact voice to use, one where there is no judgment or bias.

I was chatting with a few other moms recently, and we got into the conversation about how and when to start talking to our children about sex. I told them what I did and what seemed to work for my children. I do not believe in "The Talk" as a one-time event; instead it's an ongoing conversation. Years ago, when my children were three and five years old, we sat down with a book on sexuality (more along the lines of "where do babies come from"). I read the book ahead of time so I would know, while we were reading and one of them had a question, if that answer would be addressed in the book or not and also to know where in the book to skip ahead to if needed. I sat down with both of my daughters together; I know some parents cringe at the idea of having a younger sibling listen in. I'm sure to some extent Cindy absorbed that it was an intimate conversation, and I was willing to have it. I do believe she just enjoyed the sound of my voice because she was three; she wasn't so interested in the topic at the time, and it all just went over her head. Marcia, on the other hand, soaked it in like a sponge.

If your children are already hitting puberty, don't worry if you haven't already started the conversations. Just start now. This talk is not just penis in vagina and "birds and the bees" stuff, but it's about puberty and the changes that their bodies are going/going to go through. There's a lot of stuff happening to those little bodies. Think about your own puberty. Do you recall your first wet dream? Did anyone talk to you before it happened? If not, were you freaked out? Do you remember your first period? Did anyone talk to you before it happened? If not, did you think you were dying? We can save our children from the fear that is sometimes associated with these mundane, harmless facts of life.

Parents Judging Other Parents

From time to time, my former editor Charlie Glickman would send suggestions for blog posts to me and other Sexy Mamas bloggers. The following is one I received:

"I was chatting with a friend the other day about talking with children about sex, and she mentioned something interesting. Part of her resistance to doing so, despite her awareness of the value of it, is her concern that she'll have to deal with the fallout if her child passes the information along to other children, who will then tell their parents."

As a mom who does speak openly and honestly about sex and all kinds of other stuff with her children, I understand this parent's hesitation completely. Breaking it down, the situation above seems to me to be about two separate issues:

1. The shame a parent could feel if their child tells the truth to a friend whose parents are too scared to be honest themselves

2. A problem of communication where this other parent doesn't want to be TRUTHFUL with their child about sex topics

Now when it comes to the first issues (to shame), I know shame; I grew up Catholic, and I learned the best way to control others is through shame and guilt, right? Isn't that how most religions control which behaviors are "acceptable" and which aren't? But it's not just religion that shames people—we do it to each other so easily. Shame and righteousness have become such a big part of American culture. We're all familiar with the various forms it comes in: from shaming sexually interested adults and labeling them "promiscuous"[28] to shaming people for falling in love and wanting to be intimate with a partner, unless they are heterosexual and married to each other. So, in terms of talking to your children, be not afraid. Just breathe and know the truth is not hurting your child. Know that the shame others try to put on you cannot stick if you simply acknowledge that it's someone else's shame, not yours. If you cannot be shamed, then the shame has no power over you!

For the second issue, the truth is so important. There are lots of things to be honest with your children about, and it's bigger than just sex. We lie to our children to control their behavior in lots of ways (Santa?). However, lots of children will feel hurt or betrayed when they find out the truth. Ultimately, all children will figure out the truth—depending on the topic, some might be in their teens when it happens—but the truth will come out, nonetheless. Really, I want to be the person to give my children real, honest information now, such that they will come to me for the tough topics later. I want to make these conversations easy and commonplace, so it's just talk and no big deal. Given that there is so much misinformation out there, I want to be a source that's real.

Children are going to hear lots of information on the playground or elsewhere if we don't address it first. Here's an example of talking about tough issues. We were listening to music in the car and JLo's song "I'm Into You" came on. There is a hook in the refrain where she sings:

"When I look into your eyes, it's over
You got me hooked with your love controller.
I'm trippin' and I could not get over
I feel lucky like a four-leaf clover."

Having heard this song over and over, my girls finally asked, "What does *trippin'* mean?" I have to be honest; it escaped me a bit how to answer this. I was trying to think of what various dictionaries would say. So, I bought myself some time and asked what they thought. They wanted to know if she literally was stumbling, but they didn't think that was right. I told them it's possible that's what the songwriter meant, but that *trippin'* also had another interpretation. "When someone is on drugs or alcohol, their reality is altered; some people call that *trippin*.'" My daughters had no further questions at this point, but I'm sure the lyrics of other songs where an artist references *trippin'* were being re-cataloged in their brains. My point is this: it's okay to tell them the truth about sex or any other topic if you are doing so with love and understanding. Innocence is a concept that some adults idealize when it comes to the topics of children and sexuality, but it's a concept that doesn't suit the real education of our children. Also please notice, I let my children drive this conversation; I didn't actually have to define what I thought a "love controller" was.

Lots of parents tell me they would *never* want their children to do what they themselves did as teens. I always want to ask, "Why not? Didn't you turn out okay?" When your children are growing up, why not talk about the decisions you made, why you made them, and why you would have done things differently (if you would)? Let's not rely on the implied "do as I say, not as I do" philosophy as a way to influence our children's behavior. Talk to them with love about why they should do the things you want them to, not simply "because I'm the mother/father/teacher/authority figure." Most of us know from experience it doesn't work best that way. Kids want to understand why. They may follow your direction for a while, but eventually they will seek answers on their own and this will likely expose your untrue words.

Don't allow other parents to shame you about your parenting. Continue to be honest with your children. Do so with love and understanding. Your children will appreciate it in the long run.

Covering STIs

I went in for an annual OB/GYN check-up. The subsequent conversation between me and my daughter underscores how important it is to be up front . . . and how the conversation can be no big deal but may have a huge impact on the relationship with your child.

School was not yet back in session where I live so, like lots of mothers who didn't have childcare, I needed to take my two daughters with me to the appointment. The girls planned to wait for me in the waiting room, but once my name was called Marcia asked if she could come in. I said not this time, and she was okay with that. Next year . . . maybe.

Because of my career, I always have the most interesting conversations with my doctor. At this visit, we talked about teens and the preferred methods of birth control (my OB/GYN said the intrauterine device [IUD] was recommended because it doesn't require irresponsible teens to try to remember to take a pill on time every day). When we were finished, I decided to get a full STI panel done.

When it was time to go to the lab for the bloodwork portion of the tests, Marcia asked if she could come in for the blood draw as well. I said okay.

While we were sitting there waiting for the phlebotomist to come and draw my blood, and because she didn't know what I was at the lab for in the first place, Marcia asked, *"Are you getting allergy tests done?"*

Me: "No, I'm here to get an STI screening."

Marcia: "What's an STI?"

Me: "Sexually Transmitted Infections."

Marcia: "Who did you have sex with?"

Me: (just give her a look)

Marcia: "Oh." (half smiles) "But you don't want to have any more babies. Your tubes have been tied."

Me: "Having your tubes tied just means you can't get pregnant. It doesn't prevent me from getting an STI if I have sex."

Huge pause as she seemed to contemplate something or formulate her next question.

Meanwhile, the phlebotomist had entered the room. The young woman looked at me sideways and asked, "You talk to your daughter about this stuff?" I explained that I was a sex educator, and I would much rather talk to my daughters about everything related to sex instead of having them find out at the playground on their own. She shared with me how awesome she thought that was because she had a baby when she was fourteen years old. She said no one talked to her, and she was curious what all the fuss was about. Now that her own daughter was a teenager, this mother wants to talk to her daughter about everything too, so hopefully her daughter doesn't find herself in the same situation.

It's okay for parents to talk openly and honestly about STI testing. There are even apps I discovered and use that give people tools to safeguard themselves. The topic of STIs is just one aspect—but an important one—of a greater list of human sex and sexuality topics to cover. Each of you is the best judge of your child's mental and emotional preparedness for these topics. Just don't let your fear cloud your judgment as to when to tackle the topic. Discussing various aspects of human sexual behavior with your tweens and teens doesn't mean they will take action; it gives them information to process. Think of it this way: when someone tells YOU about something new, do you go right out and do it? Besides, how many children really want to do the same sorts of things their own parents do? You could use the "uncool" impression to your advantage.

My Marcia is a little know-it-all anyway, but I think she really appreciates the fact that she and I talk about things most parents don't. She understands what a huge part of life these topics are and has no interest in taking part at least for now. In this situation, she got to hear from the phlebotomist herself the cause and effect of having no one to talk to about sex when she was young. It was also beneficial for my daughter to hear that from another person besides me. Sadly, this woman didn't have someone there for her to be honest about things. I plan to change that for my Marcia; I want to be there for her when she does begin to have an interest in sex and let her know (leading by example as her divorced/single mother) that STI testing is an important part of setting the foundation for healthy adult sexuality.

Kids Sing the Darndest Things

I was driving my daughters and their friends home from school one day and had the radio on. The station played Rihanna's song "S & M." It was very popular at the time, so they immediately started singing. I bit my tongue while I drove, fully aware that the three girls knew all of the lyrics to this song and were singing at the top of their lungs. But I didn't say a word.

A few days later, I was again riding in the car with my daughters. Rihanna's song came on the radio again and the girls started singing it loud and proud:

I may be bad, but I'm perfectly good at it
Sex in the air, I don't care, I love the smell of it
Sticks and stones may break my bones
But chains and whips excite me
Na na na
Come on, come on, come on
I like it-like it

When the song ended, I asked my daughters if they knew what the song was about. Cindy answered right away,

Cindy: "It's about sex."

Me: "Well, the song is called 'S & M.' The 'S' stands for sadism and the 'M' stands for masochism."

Cindy: "What do those words mean?"

Me: "Those are words that roughly mean inflicting pain on someone or having someone inflict pain on you."

Marcia: "But what does S & M have to do with sex?"

Me: "It's funny because most people think S & M is about sex. S & M isn't always just about sex. Sometimes it's about taking control or giving up power. Or sometimes it's about pleasure and pain.

Marcia: "How can sex have anything to do with pain?"

Me: "Well, have you ever been spanked and instead of hurting it actually felt kinda good?"

Marcia: (chuckled and smiled) "Yeah."

And that was it. I usually start the conversation by asking a question, seeking to find out how much they know. But I allow the girls to drive the conversation as far as how much they want to know. Then I try to answer as best I can with one sentence.

This very frank conversation with them is intended to be simply information sharing. I'm doing this with my seven- and eight-year-olds, but I think they get it because we've been talking about this stuff for a while now. If your children are older, it's not too late. You will probably be surprised by what they do already know. I guess the dialog above is also an example of how to start such a conversation with your children. I'm not saying it is always easy, just that it gets easier with practice. And please note, these conversations are not about anatomy and physiology or pregnancy/STI prevention or reproductive biology alone. It's about the stuff we encounter on a daily basis while living our lives. If we can just be honest with our children, they can begin to understand the intricacies of sex and sexuality. So many adults I talk to wish their own parents would have been comfortable talking to them when they were children. Well, here is your chance to do the right thing for your kids. When we speak about these topics openly and honestly, our children won't have that same complaint. Bigger, more complex conversations will come, I'm sure. But having these little chats, early and often, make those that will come later easier.

As for Marcia's comprehension of the spanking aspect, some of you may have similar memories. Personally, I recall birthdays growing up where each child had to go through "the spanking machine": the birthday child had to crawl on his or her hands and knees through the legs of the other children and get one spanking along the way from each child. Or another variation was to get the same number of spanks for your age (see also: Core Erotic Theme in the next chapter).

As for me, I enjoy the power and control aspect. At our elementary school, every parent is required to fill a slot in traffic duty to make traffic run smoother for child drop-off and pick-up. This has to be one of my favorite parent volunteer opportunities because I get to boss other people around. There are always parents who don't follow the rules when arriving at school, and I'm pretty good at whipping them into line. For a while, I joked about dressing up as a dominatrix to do traffic duty at our school. I would have if I didn't think it would cause too much trouble. Like I said, sometimes S & M is not always about sex.

Consent

Setting boundaries is a way of caring for myself. It doesn't make me mean, selfish, or uncaring because I don't do things your way. I care about me too.

~ Christine Morgan, author

Consent: *The importance of boundaries, learning ownership for your own body, embracing and exercising the ability to say "no," and being able to accept "no" for an answer.*

Consent as a concept surrounding sex and sexuality has been receiving a lot of press lately, from consent laws on campuses to the perception that people are "asking for it" to any number of issues surrounding the confusion and misunderstanding of what consent really is and looks like. We do a terrible job of teaching about consent. Why is consent so important? After infancy, we absolutely should be permitted to maintain our own bodily autonomy and agency until we are ready to invite another person into our world. Our personal space is sacred, and adults should respect that space. Learning about consent is crucial, and it is a skill that builds throughout our lifetimes; think how important it is to be able to accept or to say "no" at age five, then age fifteen, then age twenty-five. Those skills one learns at five years old are transferable into adulthood. And that is vitally important for us to have healthy relationships.

Learning About Boundaries

Most children have a very good sense of boundaries. Our job as adults is just to help our children gain an understanding of who they are, what they are, and how far they can go. Some children need more space than others. Too often adults exert adult-like social standards on to children in social settings.

Children learn how and when it is safe to exert their boundaries through us. If they are forced to do something they don't want to at three years old, think about what could happen when they are thirteen and their boundaries are being tested. Will they do what they don't want to because that's what they have been coached or taught to do? Extend that to when they are twenty-three. Children need to learn how to express and exert boundaries when they are very young, so it is easier for them to do that when they are older.

One of my more hardline philosophies relating to consent is **if you can't talk about it, you probably shouldn't be doing it**. There are many articles teaching consent on the internet. One of my favorites is by Andrew Smiler of The Good Men Project. In his article, "Consent 102: Clarifying the Gray Spaces,"[29] he describes three ways of making sure there is no gray area when obtaining permission to proceed with sexual contact. The author makes a fine point: "If you're not comfortable saying it out loud—whether it is about permission to cuddle, kiss, or penetrate—then you're not ready to do it." A lot of people are not going to want to hear this type of message, but this philosophy could be part of a parent's teaching arsenal as well.

Children need guidance from their parents with things as simple as saying "no" when words are not yet possible.

I'll give you an example, one that was the eye-opener for me. My mother and sister came to visit me in 2011, and they brought along her daughter, my niece who was sixteen months old. My niece hadn't seen me in almost a year, and she was a little apprehensive when she first saw me (I look very similar to my sister). I squatted down to her height from a few feet away and in an excited voice said, "Come here and give me a hug!" She moved closer to mama and held on to my sister's leg very tightly. I realized at that moment this was her preverbal way of telling me, "No." I said, "Okay, that's fine. You don't want to give me a hug right now, that's okay. Just know that when you're ready to give me a hug, I'll take one." My mother, standing nearby, said, "Oh, just grab her and give her a hug." A reply from a typical grandma. I replied to my mother, "No, she is telling me she doesn't want a hug from me right now. I'm not going to force her." I recall situations with my own children as they were growing up; my mother-in-law would sort of pout if my children didn't immediately go into her arms, and she would ask them in a mock-hurt voice, "Don't you recognize your grandma?" I could never put my finger on why that bothered me, and then it hit me—it was using guilt to coerce my children into doing something they didn't want to. Come on, adults! You're the grown up. Don't try to bully children to do something they aren't comfortable doing. You are not entitled to give a hug to other people just because someone else wants one, right? It's not cool.

Do you know what teaching consent to your children looks like? Did you know it starts even when your child doesn't yet have the language to actually say "no"? Holding a parent's leg and refusing to give a hug to another person is an example of a child exercising their boundaries. You should not be undermining that.

Not everyone agrees with me; I have gotten push back about this. This question came to me:

> Shouldn't children be encouraged to move beyond their "comfort zone?" I think if a parent says go ahead and hug Aunt Carol, that's teaching a child to be forthcoming and affectionate and to appreciate those close to them. It's part of good manners, in a way. If I am seeing this incorrectly, I'd love to be educated. I perceive parents who allow their children to hide behind their legs as "coddling" them, not raising them. "Raising them" is a good phrase: Raise them up to reach a higher bar, or standard. Teach them to take some risks (hugging Aunt Carol is a tiny one!) and to push boundaries a bit. Otherwise, they will grow up in fear.

I don't have answers for this as much as I have questions. I guess the more appropriate question goes back to the adult, "Do you like to be pushed beyond your comfort zone when it comes to your own personal space?"

What is the harm in letting the child go to Aunt Carol on their own timeline? To peel them off your leg, isn't that telling them they have to do this thing they really don't want to? Fast forward to twelve years old . . . twenty-two years old . . . what message are we telling children? That they don't have agency over their bodies? No harm is done to have Aunt Carol say, "When you're ready to give me a hug, I'll be here to give you one." No guilt trip. No anger. Just love.

Why do adults have to judge children for their insecurity and force them through that discomfort? Some children are more sensitive than others—that's okay. Is "coddling" them a bad thing when it comes to making sure children know they can choose whom they want to show affection to or not? Is it a bad thing to teach children that they don't have to give a hug or a kiss to a gramma they haven't seen in a while and might be a little scared? I don't think so. Mister Rogers once said[30], "One of the first things a child learns in a healthy family is trust." Where do children learn that they can choose to say "no" if not in the safety of their own home?

I think children might have more fear if they keep getting pushed into doing things they don't want to do. Do children who are pushed to do things they don't want to hold on tighter longer? Do the ones who are allowed to have a little bit of say as to whom they do and don't kiss/hug gain more confidence faster? I don't have the answers to that, but I do know that healthy families, children, and adults appreciate support and love more than intimidation, fear, bullying, forcing, etc. Besides, this thing about manners and being polite? They are social constructs, and the "coddling" perceived by some is caring by others. I agree about health risks, but when it comes to a child's autonomy, I'm not willing to play with that. Children deserve to be protected, supported, and have their feelings validated.

Mixed Messages

We give our children many mixed messages. Adults lecture children about "stranger danger"—the belief that someone unknown to them would do them physical or emotional harm—and yet we make children hug grandma or friends of the family even as they shy away. This is sort of a crazy thing. Consider the statistics: 93 percent of juvenile sexual assault victims know their attacker[31]. It's not the stranger that causes harm most often. Unwittingly, we could be grooming our own children to stay silent and do things they might not otherwise want to because we've coached them to ignore their own boundaries under the guise of being "polite." It's not much further when we tell girls and women to "smile." These mixed messages add to the confusion children feel already while growing up.

Saying "No" and Accepting a "No"

It seems in the US, consent is something a lot of parents overlook when they talk to their children. They don't seem to think about consent as something that they need to teach about as it relates to sex, but it is very important for children to learn how to say "no" and how to accept a "no" when someone gives them one.

Charlie Glickman, one of my mentors, has been working in the field of sexuality for many years. He wrote:[32]

> "While I'm not a parent, I've certainly watched a lot of people raising children, and I think it's pretty obvious that learning how to respond to a 'no' without pushing is something that takes consistent and regular practice. It's not something that just happens with people, any more than it happens with dogs. It takes a lot of work, and it's not easy to do. And unfortunately, the behaviors that seem so minor when we're little become really annoying when we grow up, also rather like dogs. With all of the mixed messages we get about boundaries, communication, and gender rules, is it any surprise that so few people manage it?"

This is a tough one for lots of parents. Children learn from our examples. If we are not consistent with our "no," then children learn that "no" is up for negotiation. Parents are guilty of giving lots of answers to children that don't mean what they intend. To say "no" when we mean, "not now," "later," or "maybe" isn't teaching the child what "no" means. Sometimes parents allow children to nag them until they break down and give in. That also gets children to believe that an initial "no" can be changed. Some children use parents or other adults against each other and shop for the answer they want; one parent's "no" is ignored because the other parent said "yes." You know the drill. Why is this important? Not listening to or accepting a "no" could lead to problems in the future.

Do No Harm

The motto "do no harm" to someone else is also critically important to teach a child. This point ties into the next section of the five building blocks about respect. Think about this in terms of when kids are roughhousing or tickling each other, if it doesn't feel good, they must stop. If you're roughhousing and someone is getting hurt, then obviously somebody needs to stop. The same goes for tickling. If someone is tickling and it's too much, somebody needs to stop as well.

The "ah-ha!" moment for me about this came once while tickling my own children. It was as if I could see things from their perspective; if you are a child being tickled and you want the tickler to stop, how do you get them to do so when they are so much bigger and stronger than you are? I stopped tickling my children and got serious for a moment and explained to them that tickling for us would become a game of "stop and go." If I were doing the tickling and they wanted me to stop, then they just needed to say "stop," and I would honor that and freeze and stop. I would not proceed until they said, "go."

How much more fun the game became for them when they would say "stop," I would freeze, and while I was holding that position, they would catch their breath, get a big grin on their faces and say, "go." This builds trust. I respect their wishes and stop when they tell me to stop. This is not about me. Tickling, as much as any fun activity, is supposed to be fun for everybody involved and if they're not having fun, we must stop.

When I have given this example in the past, adults told me how much this resonated with them. They too had an uncle or cousin who would not stop when they wanted them to. As a result, that relative or family friend became dreaded. One woman told me, "I had an uncle who would hold me down and tickle me as a small child even after I was screaming and crying for him to stop. I never liked him." None of these adults shared with me if they told anyone how they felt as a child when they were a child. There are so many "feeling words" that come to my mind if I put myself in the position of that child: alone, scared, unsupported. Crossing this boundary can lead to terrible feelings for a child.

Adults learn consent, boundaries, and respect through experiences when they are young and are key components for anyone to learn. It's not okay to learn that you must sacrifice your bodily integrity for love.

Cuddle as a Lesson in Consent

The most important lessons about sex are not the "how-tos" for sexual positions about which people normally think, but . . .

In the previous section on communication, I wrote about attending my first Cuddle Party; there are lots of people who do not know or understand the concept of a Cuddle Party—most think it's a strange sort of sex party. How stressful it must be to assume that simple snuggling and cuddling has to lead to sex. I am grateful for all I have learned while studying the range of behaviors within sexology, without which I might never know really how truly wonderful it can be to practice your boundaries of consent and ask for what you want.

What did I get out of it? I got a wonderful night to wear my warmest, most comfy flannels to do a three-person spoon, Tour-de-France style (the one in the front goes to the back of the line)—cuddles, back rubs, back scratches, hand massages, and the like. And I wasn't required to touch or be touched by anyone with whom I did not want to engage. Think slumber parties when you were a kid. Lots of people were in jammies (except no one dipped a sleeping person's hand in water or put water-soaked bras in the freezer like they did at sleepovers when I was a kid). It was a bunch of acquaintances completely clothed and hanging out with the intention of being present, holding space, and honoring (or denying, if appropriate) requests for human contact. Such a beautiful thing! Now can you understand the smile on my face?

In 2013, during an attempt to open a Snuggle House in Madison, Wisconsin, the assistant city attorney, Jennifer Zilavy said, "There's no way that (sexual assault) will not happen. No offense to men, but I don't know any man who wants to just snuggle."[33] It seems like this viewpoint is definitely offensive to men. As I said about communication, while I know many men do not have the pleasure of experiencing massage without the pressure for things to move into more sexual behaviors, I know plenty of men who know what snuggles are and who don't try to drive the contact to sexual behavior. To believe all massages should be foreplay is a failure in our education system to teach about what sexuality is and is not *and* a failure to teach about communication, consent, respect, pleasure, and even fantasy.

The things no one talks about are exactly the things people should talk about.

Enthusiastic/Active Versus Passive Consent

Consent is not that difficult of a concept to grasp. You have to admit how important it is when you think of how it influences our children and how they will interact with others as they grow up. There are kids who enjoy "the forbidden" more than others; what they don't realize sometimes is the trouble they could get into or the consequences of their actions. They need a clear understanding of boundaries, consent, respect for the word "no," and to pay attention to the body language of others. When a person freezes or gets quiet, it is a good idea to stop and check in and see how the person is feeling. What does get confusing is the concept of active/enthusiastic or passive consent. The answer is teaching to look for an active or enthusiastic "yes" is when to proceed (really with anything in life). How do you "prove" one has obtained active or enthusiastic consent? It's the situation where you have both partners afterward saying, "I want do that again!" or "When can we do that again?"

After adults have more experience with choosing active consent, they learn how to move into instances of passive consent. Passive consent is something to discuss with your children as well, but often it's not the best choice for them. This is deciding *not* to decide or going with the flow. The prefrontal cortex of adolescent teen brains—the area of the brain where decision making, discernment, and judgment originate—aren't fully developed until late teens/early twenties. Deciding not to decide, or allowing the other person to form the decision, is when a person could get into trouble with peer pressure or mob mentality. But as an adult, passive consent may not always be a bad thing. Your spouse or partner may want to have sex with you and you're not so excited, but you're willing to go along with the idea. You say, "okay," and then when you get going you might find you like it quite a bit, but it wasn't where you started. So, in some ways passive consent is different and it's not bad. But this isn't the type of consent teens and young adults should be looking for; crucial situations like deciding to have sex for the first time or when they are in a vulnerable space (engaging with a partner after drinking or doing drugs) require active consent.

The Mating Call of the Drunken Heterosexual Female

Here's something you may or may not realize: women of any age are not permitted to appear interested in sex. It's also not acceptable for women to be overtly sexual. To some of you, that is not new news.

It begins when we are young. Some parents look the other way when their sons touch themselves, but daughters for the most part get shamed, told "don't touch," and redirected. This starts the detachment women experience between their minds and their genitals. This is the way it has been for a lot of girls, but I see a problem with that; the basic, innate sexuality that is supposed to be part of their lives becomes separated from the rest of their personality Take these girls and fast-forward to adulthood. Some women are not aware when they are aroused. Some women don't know what turns them on. Some women have never had an orgasm.

Once girls become adults, our society does not want women to show any interest in sex unless it's in a married, heterosexual relationship, but even within that narrow definition, there is an expectation once you do get married that you get busy baby makin'. Anything else is labeled "deviant" (that's a horrible term!). Fast-forward to advanced age; our society has a gross-out factor thinking about "older" women being sexual. Again, this is so sad and so negative.

Because of this cultural view of female sexuality, women have adapted to get what they want and preserve their persona. There is a phenomenon that I have observed in multiple heterosexual settings. I call it the *"Drunk American Girl Mating Call,"* a behavior exhibited by women who seek the attention, most often sexual attention, of the opposite sex. Everyone, especially men, seem to recognize this behavior without even realizing what is happening. Picture this: You are in a bar. It's getting late. There's a group of women, maybe a ladies' night out or bachelorette party. Most times there's alcohol involved. Inevitably, one of the women in the group is getting a little tipsy . . . she puts her arm(s) in the air, tips her head back, eyes closed, and lets out a "WHOOOOOO!!" That's the Drunk American Girl Mating Call. Men zero in on that woman as if she is the weak one in the herd. It's a deliberate announcement that one is ready to party, but it can be interpreted in many ways. Most clearly, it sends out a message that this woman is a little drunk and more receptive to being hit on as opposed to another woman who is sitting in the corner sipping sparkling water.

This happens because it's not acceptable for women to be sexual beings. If a woman does engage in sexual behavior while drunk, she has a built-in excuse for it: "OMG, I was so drunk last night." This insulates her image and most importantly her reputation. She's still a "good girl." Again, the issue I have is this: It's not okay for women to act sexually aware. It's not okay for women to dress overtly sexy. It's not okay for women to talk in a sexually suggestive way. Given all of this, what are the alternatives for women who are interested in engaging in potentially nonfamily-forming behavior? Evidently, the Drunk American Girl Mating Call.

I'd like to see changes in what's acceptable in terms of gender roles for a number of dating behaviors. Now keep in mind, I am not calling for women to do these things every time, all the time. I want it to be acceptable for any gender to do these things. Here's my ideal: It's okay for anyone to initiate conversation with a person they find attractive. It's okay for anyone to ask another person out or ask for their contact information. It's okay for anyone to plan a date. And by extension, it's okay for anyone to initiate sexual contact if they so desire. Ideally, there would be a give-and-take with both partners equally interested and involved in moving things forward maybe even to the point of a relationship. But it would also be okay if a person doesn't want a relationship. I'd like to see more consent and respect on behalf of both parties as well.

It should be acceptable for women to be sexual beings—to feel sexual, to want sexual satisfaction, to speak up for what they want. As it is now, it's not going to be handed over willingly; we must speak up for what is best for all women.

If She's Not Having Fun You've Got to Stop

My training as a sexologist makes me aware of people, things, and situations around me that have a sexual component to them. The latest is a situation that I've observed for a while now, and I could not put my finger on it as to why it concerned me.

Let me explain:

I have a guy friend who is a divorced dad of a nine-year-old girl. As the daughter has been growing up, the two of them became very close. This father/daughter combo is very loving; they sit quietly with each other affectionately. She is very protective (possessive?) of her father as he now ventures into the dating scene. And like most dads, he is extremely aware of her changing prepubescent body and is nervous about the conversations he will need to have with her about the same. It's touching for me to see this relationship really.

Over time, I have seen that this father/daughter pair wrestles a bit, like playful roughhousing. She'll say something to tease him, and he'll quickly swoop in and put his arm around her shoulders and squeeze her in to him as she squeals with pleasure. Or she'll answer something that she knows is wrong as they work on homework together, and he'll give her "the knuckle," a move that sends her into fits of giggles as he pokes his knuckle into her side or back.

While I also see them when they aren't being rough, this past weekend it struck me why I've been struggling with this roughhousing—he has not started having conversations with her about dating (his own), divorce, love, relationships, puberty, etc., yet I begin to wonder, will this roughness become a familiar feeling that she will seek out in her adult romantic relationships? There are times when he is pretty rough with her, not that she's a shrinking violet or anything; she's not. She is a confident, happy, seemingly secure little girl. I'm sure she is thrilled at the 100% attention and affection from her father. What little girl wouldn't be? When we are young adults, and even in childhood we are developing what Jack Morin in his book, *The Erotic Mind,*[34] calls the Core Erotic Theme (CET).

> *"Your Core Erotic Theme begins its long evolution during childhood and is first sketched out in fantasies and daydreams you probably don't remember. Because these early images almost certainly grew out of impulses and interests considered inappropriate for children,*

they were veiled in secrecy. Even now you probably still keep certain ultra-personal turn-ons—those that spring from your CET– hidden from other people and quite possibly even from yourself."

If I were the dad in this situation, I would remind her that I love her unconditionally and explain that our roughhousing is play. Most importantly, that she has permission to say "no thanks" if she's really not in the mood or "stop" when it's too much. I would also tell her that as she gets older, she should always feel comfortable speaking up whenever she doesn't want to be touched. Whether it's a slobbery kiss from a grandparent or tickling from a cousin, or with whomever she is playing, that she should always feel comfortable saying "no" without worrying about hurting the other person's feelings. And that whomever she loves shouldn't play rough with her if she doesn't like it. Ever.

For this chat, I am reminded of a message from a blog I once read.[35] In it, the dad tells his two-year-old son, who is roughhousing with a little girl/friend, "If she's not having fun, you have to stop." Another nugget of wisdom here is that the message is clear: Adults should note that a child "doesn't need to know what sex or rape is to know what a partner is. If your partner isn't having fun, you stop." The same is true for mature adults and young adults alike.

All this ties in nicely with two incredibly important concepts: CONSENT and PLEASURE. It is age-appropriate—for *any* age—to learn about consent and boundaries to lay a solid foundation onto which a parent builds future talks about sex and sexuality. This is one example of talking to your children about sexuality in a way that has *nothing* to do with penises or vulvas but is just as important, if not more so. It is also important to teach children early on that if it doesn't feel good, you must stop. Those early sexual experiences that our children will have when they become young adults should have deeply entrenched messages that pleasure should be had by all, and it if doesn't feel good, you have to stop. Any message which denies pleasure as part of the equation sets our children up for potential pain in the future. There are just too many news articles of boys raping unconscious girls, some examples here,[36], here[37] and here;[38] presumably they don't understand how important consent and pleasure are for themselves and their partner(s) in a sexual interaction. We cannot deny pleasure anymore. See the chapter on pleasure for further information on this subject. I have devoted a whole chapter on pleasure alone.

Respect

You yourself, as much as anybody in the entire universe, deserve your love and affection.

~ Buddha

Respect: *Having a healthy respect for self and for others, learning a healthy body image and being okay with nakedness, and extending the concept of "do no harm" (along with consent), and a word or two about "virginity."*

Respect is something many people recognize is as important as being human, but how does respect relate to building healthy sexuality? Being able to connect with others is crucial to having healthy relationships in general, but it all begins with having a healthy respect for yourself and your own body first. Then we need to learn to have respect for others, which enables us to have good relationships with others.

Over the past years, I have noticed a lack of respect in our culture—a very wide spectrum of disrespectful behaviors toward people of different genders, races, sexual orientation or sexualities. This is not just violence against women, it's violence against anything "other." Some examples include creating drama around transgender people using public bathrooms, the behavior of the rapists of Steubenville and Vanderbilt, the rapes in India, legislation attempts to control women's reproductive choices (which affects lower socioeconomic classes harder than it does the wealthy), and forgetting that marriage is about love, not just religion or procreation or wealth. There is so much disrespect directed at others that it feels like a distraction or redirection, paying attention to things outside of oneself and outside of one's control.

Respect for others includes acceptance and acknowledgment of everyone, as well as support for any "other" (i.e., gay, lesbian, bisexual, transgender). I talk to my children about how what other people do sexually is none of my business. It's none of anyone else's business either. They understand this plainly. The only people who should be concerned with another person's sexuality are the ones engaging with that person directly. What exactly do I mean? It shouldn't make any difference to you what genitals I have in my pants *unless* I'm having sex with you. Simple enough, right? Lots of people get really hung up on that though. Think of how silly it is to be upset by that. What difference does it really make?

It's a really messed up "perfect storm" brewing right now. Everyone wants to have great relationships with others. But how does one develop this in a culture that tells girls to flaunt "what your mama gave you" and boys that their sexual desires cannot be controlled? Being a problem solver, I want to *fix* it because this aspect of our society seems really broken. So, let's look at the individual components of respect.

Respect for Self

There is an old Bible verse[39] that says, "your body is a temple;" and some believe we are all made in God's image. Regardless of your religious affiliation, it is important for children to learn a healthy body image. This includes being okay with nakedness because the human body is beautiful and utilitarian. Children do not have any shame or guilt around their bodies when they are very young. Note how lots of them walk around naked. They are proud of their bodies. Shame and guilt are learned from what they see and hear the adults around them do or say. Adults are the ones who sexualize the naked body. If you have ever spent a significant amount of time around naked bodies, you eventually notice the nudity is no longer a big deal.

A Healthy Body Image

Self-Love: This is acceptance of who you are, what you want and need, and your body image—an important part of the respect-for-self-puzzle. Having a good deal of love and respect for yourself is important for men and women. Children just won't get the same type of experience until their parents have a healthy body image, too. I'm sorry, but all the diet talk, body shaming, and unhealthy attitudes that parents have toward bodies (their own and others' bodies) get absorbed by the children around you. They're figuring things out just as much as we are. Since I've written about my experience—having gone to the Kabuki Spa in San Francisco many times now—I have a much more realistic and healthy understanding of "me," and the experience has helped me to develop a previously unknown amount of respect and appreciation for self and the beauty of others.

Look at how much you rely on or assign value to the opinions of others to make your own decisions. Many girls and young women don't realize it's okay to pursue what they want. They tend to let others decide things for them and don't speak up about what they want or need. Some would rather do what their partner wants and not cause waves in the relationship. I've had grown women friends who would rather say nothing than risk losing a partner. A few of these women eventually hit a breaking point where they couldn't do that anymore. Looking at divorce rates it seems obvious: spending so much time trying not to lose someone, you may lose yourself in the process.

Sometimes I hear about young people engaging in sexual behavior mindlessly. It's as if they are doing it to get attention or for acceptance. Some do it for the notoriety or to be popular. Contrary to the belief that a single-sex school keeps kids innocent longer, this happens whether it is an all-girl[40] or all-boy school. Remember back to when you were in school—if you were sexually active at a young age, do you recall the reasons why you did what you did? What advice would you give your younger self?

Respect for Others

"Do no harm" is a concept I touched upon in the previous section about consent, and it fits here as it relates to interacting with other people. The Dalai Lama once said, "Be kind whenever possible. And it is always possible." And in terms of guiding children about how to deal with others, one of the best bits of advice you can give any child or adult is to "ask before you touch." It is respectful to assume others don't want to be touched, but you can always ask, whether it is a handshake or a hug. My parents always told me, "Do unto others as you would have them do unto you." Someone should have the decency to ask first.

I have experienced plenty of push back on the ask-before-you-proceed point, especially as it relates to sex and chemistry! Men and women both have strong opinions about this one. I did too . . . back before I went back to school to study human sexuality. This point alone (people wanting the ability just to *take* what they want or to be *taken*) I get it, but that really works best when someone feels safe and comfortable with another person. Lots of people still believe women want to be taken without being asked—this is a very dangerous notion because without consent it can approach assault. Being able to communicate with another person about what I want, to be heard, and if necessary, to negotiate how to get that and what it looks like (consent from each of us), being respectful participants has facilitated much pleasure for both of us. Respect is crucial, and I hope every teen gets to experience that in their interactions and relationships once they get to that stage.

Examples of respect are happening everywhere, every day around our children, and parents should be mindful of how it shows up in the modeled or learned behavior of adults in the lives of our children: how we talk to our spouses or significant others; how we objectify the opposite sex; how we talk on the phone; the gossip we engage in; what we say about other parents; what we say about what's going on at school. This is a really important point because children learn what they live[41]. We can model respect for others and demonstrate that we are not above them and that everybody deserves respect.

Respect for others includes being kind to everyone, regardless of their gender expression or identity. I specify this because we can support being friends with kids who are the same gender, opposite gender, or gender fluid. Growing up can be tough, and it's perfectly fine for each of our children to see some of the issues their friends have to go through. Gender has its own challenges during adolescence, not to mention the challenges of adulthood. It's easier to empathize with someone if you know what they're going through. There is no reason for another's experience to be mystical or unknown, tying this back to communication. This goes for having conversations about puberty or growing up as well. Don't separate or treat children of different genders or children who do not identify with a specific gender differently when talking about sex topics. In their lifetimes, they will have friends and their friends will have issues. How much better will it be if your child can be compassionate because they can ask, understand, offer support, and be respectful?

Here's a challenging item for parents: encourage your children to develop friendships with the opposite gender. Try not to call every friend they have who is a different gender a "boyfriend" or "girlfriend," and instead give them retorts like "He's not my boyfriend. He's my buddy.[42]" If we can encourage nonromantic, non-sexualized relationships between children, then we encourage the ability to build good nonsexual friendships with any gendered person as adults. Lynne Griffin wrote a piece in *Psychology Today* about how having friends of the opposite gender helps our children develop their own sense of self:

> "More importantly your child gets to continue with his or her own identity development. She learns what's important to her; he learns what he finds interesting; she doesn't define herself by what a boy thinks of her. Sure, your child still identifies with what friends think but the bigger and more varied the group, the more your child has a chance to see what's best for him or her."[43]

We have the opportunity to help our children figure out what is best for them. And we can learn about their friends. As we learn about these young people growing up and figuring out who they are, here again, the best thing we can do is ask. Avery Wallace, a fifteen-year-old in California, wrote about his experience[44] of figuring out who he was. He made an excellent point. Avery said, "I was the first person and truly the only person capable of answering the 'is it a boy or girl' question—not the doctor, my parents, or anyone who thinks they know better." There are a few tools on the internet that provide a bit of valuable information about others as well. The Trevor Project's "The Spectrum"[45] and the Genderbread person[46] or Gender Elephant are tools that also work with the respect block. If we help kids understand that these things are a spectrum, it is easier to understand and accept someone who doesn't fit nicely into a label. Get to know the "other," and they aren't an "other" anymore.

On the Term Virginity

While we are on the topic of respect, I'd like to also address the term "virginity" and the issues surrounding this. Virginity is a social construct[47] that is outdated, sexist, and limited in its purview. It is defined primarily by an event: vaginal penetration by a penis. Thinking about virginity in such a narrow way doesn't acknowledge many sexual behaviors, let alone same-sex behavior. Keep in mind that same-sex play does not indicate a person identifies as "gay" or "lesbian."[48] Not only is it time to stop thinking about the definition of "sex" as just penises in vaginas, but it's also time to take back the rite of passage that becoming a sexual being is and rename this construct "sexual debut."

I think changing the word we use would minimize the emphasis on "virginity" because virginity is only one sexual behavior. Most people associate virginity with penises in vaginas, and once that milestone has occurred you are no longer a virgin. What happens when a person has their first kiss or their first blow job? Those are points on a sexual debut spectrum, but we don't acknowledge those behaviors.

Thinking about virginity as being so prized, and losing one's virginity as such a loss, is a terrible thing. No one's value should be reduced to what happens between their legs. So many girls think they are "ruined" after they have sex. Are they ruined? NO. The behaviors girls are shamed for range from kissing petting, or manual manipulation to intercourse. Their engagement may not even be sexual, but whatever it is, it gives young women a sense of shame. Even how we teach abstinence only sex education has a hand in this. Elizabeth Smart went through abstinence-only education and recalls some of the examples used in the lessons, the chewed-up piece of gum one in particular. She has said the notion that sexual activity eliminates a woman's value leaves one feeling like, "Who would ever want me now? I'm worthless."[49] Her feeling is fairly common for women who went through this type of sex ed and who have been raped.

When we continue to put so much value, stress, and emphasis on an adolescent's virginity, it has the potential to do so much damage emotionally and psychologically—especially if they did not have any choice in the timing of their sexual debut. It is empowering for a young person who was raped to be able to identify their own sexual debut on their own terms.

Can we stop putting so much value on this concept of virginity? We don't have the same value placed on boys' "virginity." Ask yourself if that's fair. Boys are victim to this virgin stigma as well; boys who are sexual are revered to some extent—they've become men. But the ones who are not sexually active become resentful and angry. In this hypersexualized society, they believe women give themselves to other men but not them. Elliot O. Rodger, the man who committed the Isla Vista murders[50] in 2014, is an example of this. He was very bitter about his virgin status because women wouldn't have sex with him.

Viewing virginity as something that only occurs in heterosexual intercourse also doesn't acknowledge same-sex debut behaviors. Are all of the definitions of "virginity" based on heterosexual activity? If so, when does a lesbian woman lose her "virginity"? When does a gay man lose his? When does somebody who's bisexual lose their virginity? Or a bigger question: Why is virginity defined by a woman's or girl's interaction with a penis?

Some young people are having unprotected anal sex because technically they remain "virgins." They do this without condoms because they know enough about reproduction to understand the woman can't get pregnant that way. This is still an activity that puts them at risk of STIs though. Yet young people don't get educated about this because some adults deny the reality that some teens have sex and educators refuse to give teens the information they need. If information about STI transmission is made available, in the event they do have sex, they can do so in a way that reduces the potential harm. But I can understand this: How many of us adults have conversations about safer sex with our partners? If we can't talk to our partners about sex, most likely we can't talk to our children about it either.

Shifting our thinking away from virginity to sexual debut allows us to mark many different events as our debut—and demand respect for ourselves in how we define it.

Change Is Good

There is a lot of good work being done right now by many different groups of people within the United States affecting positive change as it relates to sexism, racism, transphobia, and other societal ills. We do have the power to change what is not working—and the American approach to sexuality needs to change. I was living in Germany when I got to see first-hand how different American culture was around children and sexuality. At the public pool in Germany, children can splash and play while they're naked and there is no shame or reaction at all from the other adults at the pool. I can tell you there are many places in the United States where the reaction to a naked child would be a broad range—anything from rude staring or leering to a person feeling compelled to tell you to cover up your child to covering the eyes of other children nearby as if there is something shameful about a naked human body. I presume I don't need to explain to this group the negative effects on body image when people begin to internalize shame associated with their body. Of course, the United States is not the only place in the world where attitudes must change. We can be leaders for the rest of the world and show how much better a society can be when we adopt a more accepting attitude towards the sexuality of others.

Let's Get Naked

I went out for a friend's birthday and as the night went on the group got smaller and smaller, and we moved in closer. I hadn't met some of the women, and our mutual friend introduced me as The MamaSutra. One mom had a twelve-year-old daughter, and we got started talking about the book *Queen Bees and Wannabes* by Rosalind Wiseman.[51] We talked about "Girl World" and about girl's self-confidence at that age. She said she was starting to be concerned with her daughter's body image. I told her it might be an interesting exercise to go together to the Kabuki Spa (a spa in the Japantown neighborhood of San Francisco that has a communal bath. A few times a week they offer women-only days where the use of the spa is clothing optional).

Above all else, going to this spa is an exercise in self-acceptance. I can't say that any more clearly. I think there are a lot of really messed up, misogynistic aspects to American society today; the photoshopped images that we all see every day in magazines and on TV are having a tremendous negative effect on us as mothers, on young women, and on our own daughters. Our inability collectively to look in the mirror and see what's beautiful, but instead only see the flaws, reminds me of a scene in the movie *Mean Girls* (based on Rosalind Wiseman's book *Queen Bees and Wannabes*). The main character, Cady, transfers to a typical suburban high school after growing up overseas. She is totally unfamiliar with "Girl World." Three of the popular high school girls are standing in front of a mirror and, in turn, criticize their images. Then they turn to Cady with an expectant look on their faces . . . like it is her turn to criticize herself. She responds with, "*I have really bad breath in the morning.*" (http://www.youtube.com/watch?v=ZZDQYVU8o9M).

This is the kind of attitude and behavior I think needs to change, but it must start with us adult women so we can pass it on to our daughters.

I think a little more background is helpful here. In my studies at the Institute for Advanced Study of Human Sexuality, I have learned, shared, and/or discussed every aspect of human sexuality—from the simple, yet powerful impact of pure, nonsexual human touch and its importance to deeper discussions of homosexuality and heterosexuality and everything in between. Spending a day in the communal baths at a spa such as this approaches a fraction of the value one can get without enrolling in the school.

I heard about this spa initially from some former classmates. The first time I went by myself. It was completely foreign to me. I didn't realize there was a process to follow, and it was a bit unsettling to be surrounded by people who were not wearing any clothes. I found myself purposefully trying to avoid eye contact with anyone and also avoid looking at anyone in general. But then after about five or ten minutes, I got comfortable. I started to look around a bit and noticed what may seem obvious: everyone was different. Different body types, breast sizes, hips, proportions . . . everything. And after a while—and this may sound trite—I noticed each woman was beautiful! And none of them looked like they needed to photoshop anything. And eventually, I started to appreciate my own body in a way I hadn't before.

I really do think this is a tremendous experience, and I encourage women everywhere to find this opportunity. I have found a couple spas like it, and I'm sure more of these gems can be found around the country. To be clear, sex is not allowed at the Kabuki Spa. It is an upscale *joie de vivre* spa, and it is such a wonderful place to relax in a comfortable and safe space amongst women. It is a place of peace and tranquility where talking is really frowned upon because it disturbs the silence of this very serene place.

Since finding this place, I go often. I have also found it to be a wonderful bonding experience when going with my girlfriends. I have taken all of my in-from-out-of-town visiting girlfriends. Some go with a swimsuit--as I mentioned, it's clothing optional. Still, each one has gotten something different out of the experience. I think there is incredible value and empowerment in going to this spa even if you go alone for the first time. Yes, it can be difficult to get naked in front of other people, maybe even more so with your friends. I totally get that . . . I was raised in a Catholic household complete with all the requisite Catholic guilt.

I look forward to the opportunity to take my daughters to a spa like this. My daughters have heard me speak about it so highly so often that they are looking forward to their opportunity to go, but for this particular spa, they must wait until they are ten years old. I encourage all adults to take their children to a clothing-optional spa so they can see everyone has different bodies as well. I want my daughters to appreciate their bodies. I want them to love themselves. I want them to learn to honor and respect their bodies. I want to teach them to take care of themselves. And I want them to understand the real-life differences between the people we see every day and the stuff they see in the media. Soon enough they'll be in junior high and they will be living in that "Girl World." I think experiences like this will give them a good foundation of self-appreciation before they enter "Girl World." Since children emotionally track the adults in their lives and understand a whole lot more than we adults are sometimes willing to share with them, they must see this self-appreciation in us adults first.

Happy Dot Day

My daughters, Marcia (eight) and Cindy (six), and I started discussing the changes that happen to a kid's body when they go through puberty or hormone replacement therapy to change genders. We discussed all the usual stuff but in very general terms:

In kids who have a penis, a few of the changes that occur are the following: hair starts to grow around the base of the penis, hair grows under the arms and on the chest, some kids get growing pains in their bones, and eventually, hair grows above their upper lip and their voice gets deeper.

The changes in kids who have a vulva can sometimes happen up to two years earlier than for those kids who have a penis. Many times, the first change that's noticed is breast development. At the same time, the ovaries are preparing to begin ovulating. They also start to grow hair around the vulva and under their arms. The hormones that are produced in the ovaries are causing these changes. These are just a few of the many changes that occur, sometimes as early as nine years old. All of this builds up to a child getting her period for the first time.

I've heard lots of stories about daughters and moms dealing with menstruation issues—some funny, some sad. Some of my friends said their moms called it "The Curse" or apologized to them. Other women shared that their mothers didn't talk about the first menstruation with them at all. Then they feared they were dying because they were bleeding and it wasn't stopping. Can you imagine the emotional trauma of a young person who has no knowledge at all about what was happening to her body? On a lighter note, have you heard the one about the little girl who's helping her mom set the table for dinner? She goes into the bathroom and brings out the good "napkins." I am excited for when my girls make the transition from big girls to little women. Based on my own experiences with menstruation at puberty, I've tried to make it a positive thing, something to look forward to as well in this whole "growing up" experience. I told Marcia and Cindy that when they get their period for the first time, we would have a party with a present and bake a cake . . . a red velvet cake! Cindy wants a figurine on the cake of a girl using a mirror to look at her private parts. That cracked me up. She's also the one who came up with the name for the day: Happy Dot Day, a celebration like a birthday but celebrating a girl getting her period.

Besides a party, I plan to give a present as well. I heard one of my favorite Bay Area puberty educators, Ivy Chen, give a fantastic suggestion at a meeting of parents. She suggested giving the girls a small toiletry bag filled with a clean pair of underwear, one of those heating pads that you twist to activate for cramps, a sanitary pad or two, and if your school will allow it, Midol for cramps. I thought this was a fantastic idea and that's going to be the present my daughters get on their Happy Dot Day.

My children and I have talked about all of the paraphernalia that goes with the period, i.e., pads, tampons, etc. We have also had conversations about—and this might sound fairly Earth Motherish to some of you—the Diva Cup. This is not something for the squeamish, but it's very eco-friendly. One of my girlfriends tipped me off to it a couple years ago. Since I am using one, I no longer spend money on feminine products for "Aunt Flo."

If they walk in on me in the bathroom, I don't hide that time of the month from my kids (I haven't shown them *exactly* what I'm doing, but I have told them where things go and the purpose) because for the most part, it's a natural part of being an adult who menstruates. Presumably, they will be going through menstruation as well. It is okay to talk to your children about menstruation. Once you've explained things in a straightforward manner, it loses all of its scariness. As for menstruation, nearly half of the population has it, had it, or will have it in their lifetime and for a child to grow up less scared or fearful about one more bodily function is a good thing.

At One Point, I Noticed My Baby Was Growing Up

At one point, I noticed my baby was growing up! It was no surprise really. I'd known for a while. Little things kept happening—she got pretty crabby, teary, and ecstatic around the same time of the month as me, and her skin seemed to be changing. I noticed little blemishes on her face, the usual secondary sex characteristics that begin when a child starts to go through puberty.

But then one day, Marcia was sitting down on the couch wearing a lightweight, shirred top I looked over at her and noticed her little mounds starting to push through the top! I swear I did a double take. I felt like I wanted to squeal inside. Later, I pulled her aside and told her what I noticed. She had the biggest grin on her face. So, we sat down to discuss breast development and a little more about puberty.

We talked about the potential ramifications of wearing a bra. We talked about the taunting and teasing about bras and breasts that could happen at school. I told both girls that when I first got a training bra some boys used to snap the strap. It irritated me, but I never said anything to them about how much it upset me (here we have a failure of consent and respect).

I also told them about the time during my freshman year in high school when a popular boy (class president, quarterback, and dreamboat) commented about me in my cheerleading sweater. Back in those days, the letter on the sweater was stiff-as-a-board, huge, and despite my seemingly early development (those changes slowed) I was pretty flat chested in high school. At times, this stupid letter was concave! Well, this guy came up to me and asked if I had a book in my sweater. I was devastated. I didn't have a response. I held on to that embarrassment for twenty years! I told my daughters about running into him at our twenty-year class reunion. I confronted him and said, *"Say, do you remember the time you asked if I had a book in my cheerleading sweater?"* He said with a bit of sassiness, *"No, but I wouldn't be surprised if I said something like that."* I said to him, *"Well,*

I'm here to tell you . . ." (I held each of my breasts in my hands with an attitude like Teri Hatcher in a *Seinfeld* episode,[52] "*. . . they're real, and they're spectacular.*" The two guys standing there with him did a sort of a back-of-the-hand-to-their-mouths "*oh shiiii*" response. He was humbled. I felt vindicated. At hearing this story, my daughters were rolling on the floor laughing. *"MOM! Did you really?"* Yes. Yes, I did.

Anyway, back to the children. We talked some more, and I finally asked Marcia if she would be comfortable with a bra and she got so excited! I told her we would go bra shopping after school. She was literally so excited that she could not sleep that night. It was like Christmas Eve! That next day we bought three new training bras. And she was over the moon!

I delight in having these conversations with my daughters. I feel like they bring us closer together every day. I want to share my experiences with my girls. I'm sure they appreciate hearing how I felt, how I reacted, and how I wished I had reacted instead. These things are situations they may or may not be able to use in their little lives, but if it gives them the chance to think through how it was for someone else and gain a shred of wisdom from my experiences, then it's 100% worth it.

Olympic Wardrobe Malfunctions

During a broadcast of the 2012 Olympic games in London, an underwater altercation occurred during a women's water polo match between a US player and a player from Spain. The only reason we heard about it was because there are cameras below the surface of the water. So, what's the big deal about this little fight? We saw a full side view of the Spanish athlete's breast and nipple.

Twitter supposedly went NUTS. Some choice tweets were: "*I*

don't think that's legal to see a girl's boob fully exposed on the TV during an Olympic water polo game . . . "#wtf there are families watching," and *"Just saw a boob on the Olympics. Women's water polo is awesome!"* This event has been called "The Water Polo Wardrobe Malfunction."

I heard about as many people complain about seeing a breast on TV as I did people upset that it wasn't in HD. While there's a difference between sexy and sexual, this instance was neither one of these. It was simply a breast shown by accident.

Ask fans or players of water polo; this is nothing new to the sport. Something similar happened at the 2008 games as well. A Greek athlete had her left breast fully exposed, but she was above the water surface when it occurred. A friend told me about her cousin who played water polo; she said, *"If you talk to her about 'malfunctions'* she will tell you this example was innocent and tame compared to the thrills she and her teammates gave the crowd each game. She once said, "*You have to be okay with flashing your boobs to an audience if you want to play water polo."*

Lots of Americans know that Europe has plenty of nude and topless beaches. It may not come as a surprise to you then to know this "event" was not news at all in Europe. I reached out to some of my European friends. The only information available about that match was gambling and betting information. One friend's German husband said, *"German media reporting on the malfunction? [No, because] it isn't news."*

I know Europeans who think it is laughable that Americans freak out about things like this. It reminds me of 2004, when Americans freaked out over the Janet Jackson Superbowl XXXVIII "Wardrobe Malfunction." The world laughing isn't the way to go because seeing a woman's breast or nipple does not need to be a big deal. We all have them—nipples that is. We have breasts too. Some are bigger than others, some are small, some hang, some are fake, etc. There's nothing to be ashamed of in terms of our bodies. To do so sets people up for issues later in life.

It's interesting to note here that the original Olympic games were done naked! Wikipedia says (fine, I know it isn't the top authority but stay with me), "The athletes usually competed nude, not only as the weather was appropriate but also as the festival was meant to celebrate, in part, the achievements of the human body. Olive oil was used by the competitors [. . .] to keep skin smooth and provide an appealing look for the participants." These are amazing athletes competing at the international level. They are not there to titillate the viewer—more like astound the audience with their amazing feats of athleticism, sportsmanship, and awesomeness.

Boob shown on the Olympics? Children are not going to be scarred by seeing breasts. They will be more scarred by the fear and shame of the adults around them; or at the very least, entertained that you are being ridiculous and take every opportunity to point breasts out to you to see your embarrassment again.

Seriously, no USA, seeing neither the boob nor the nipple is going to scar your children. Any shame and fear you demonstrate about it probably will though.

Children Learn What They Live

This post is about how I want to instill in my children the desire to love, respect, and take care of their bodies in a way I never did when I was younger.

My girls and I watch movies together. I think of it as an exercise in media literacy; it gives us an opportunity to evaluate what is happening and discuss the messages, both direct and implied. This is how it works: we pause the movie where they have questions or there's something I think is important to point out, talk briefly, and then resume. Some of the movies we watch are things like *Bolt* or *The Incredibles*, but others have more mature situations in them like *Hitch* or *Pursuit of Happyness*. Contrary to what the Motion Picture Association of America (MPAA) practices, I personally would rather have my children see romantic comedies or movies dealing with complex relationship issues as opposed to violence. Most importantly, I am there, present, watching with them. It feels like a reality check if things in the movie get too intense.

When Marcia and Cindy were five and seven years old respectively, we started watching the movie Mean Girls. There is one scene in Mean Girls where the popular girls stand in front of a mirror and criticize their bodies: "My hairline is so weird," "I have man shoulders," and "My nail beds suck." They then look expectantly at the girl who has not been socialized in this way to join in the party.

Video clip: *Mean Girls*, "Looking in the Mirror," 2004
http://www.youtube.com/watch?v=ZZDQYVU8o9M53

I know this behavior is not unique to teen girls because I know plenty of adult women who do this to this day. Even I catch myself doing it from time to time. But I began to realize that my girls were *not* doing this to themselves . . . yet, and I thought it made sense to plan a preemptive strike.

The next time we had a bath night, I tried something new. I reminded my girls of the movie. I spoke with happiness and enthusiasm, kind of like a cheerleader's voice without the volume.

"Do you girls remember the scene in Mean Girls when The Plastics stood in front of the mirror and said bad things about their bodies?"

"Yeah."

"Well, it's sad not to like your body because you are in it for your WHOLE LIFE. We've already talked about all the wonderful things our bodies do for us. So, I want to try something different. I'm gonna stand in front of the mirror and say three things I like about my body. Do you want to try too?"

"Okay!" (The cheerleader's voice was working.)

I went first. Now keep in mind this is done with the intention of modeling positive behavior for any gender. It can be done in underwear or a swimsuit if you are not as comfortable naked. I stood in front of the full-length mirror and looked at myself. After some assessment I said, *"I like my neck, my breasts, and my legs."* Children are masterful at being able to pick up on nonverbal cues and inconsistencies, so if your children have seen you look in the mirror and criticize your body or wince when you look in the mirror, you're going to have more work ahead of you and need to do this more often to try to undo that prior impression. Or at least be more mindful of it when your children are in your zip code. You already know how well they hear you from a distant part of the house.

Marcia, who was seven at the time, stepped up next. Without hesitation, she said, "I like my lips, my eyes, and my hair." It was obvious she already knew what she liked about herself. I hope that never goes away.

Cindy, then five, was no shrinking violet either. She stepped right up to the mirror, turned from side to side, and said confidently, "I like my bweasts, my butt, and my pwivate pawts." I giggled out loud at that response, thinking to myself "Oh no you di-in't!" but I was very conscious not to make my giggle appear critical or unaccepting in any way. I told her that was so sweet. Why wouldn't those parts be her favorite parts? They're awesome and she knows they belong to her. When we finished, I told the girls I was proud of them because there are adults who can't do this exercise or they have a hard time finding things they like.

I have tried to explain to my children that when they hear other girls criticize their own bodies, it may be a result of what they have seen on TV, in magazines, in other media, or a behavior they have witnessed other women in their lives do. The people at Dove established the Dove Self-Esteem Fund and created this video that I think is fantastic to watch, especially if you have daughters.

Video: by Dove, "Beauty Pressure," 2007
http://www.youtube.com/watch?v=Ei6JvK0W60I[54]

Since that first exercise in front of the mirror with my girls, we've added other things along the way. We talk about the nonphysical qualities we appreciate in ourselves and each other, and we've talked about the features and characteristics we like about each other. It's nice to hear someone say something nice once in a while when there's not any innuendo or expectation attached.

To be totally honest, before doing this exercise with my children, I first did this mirror exercise when I was forty, and I cried. It's not easy to grow up with a true appreciation for your body, especially if you've grown up in the United States given the influences we have. My mother gives me harsh looks when I compliment my girls on their bodies. And when she does it, I understand a little more each time as to why it took me nearly forty years to accept my own body. I'm sure ride, one of the seven deadly sins) is what my Catholic mother is worried about. However, there are two top definitions of pride:

World English Dictionary
pride (prahyd), n.

1. A feeling of honor and self-respect; a sense of personal worth

2. Excessive self-esteem; conceit

Where is the boundary between one and two above? I'm sure it's something far more sinister than being able to look in the mirror and appreciate the good things you see.

I think having a healthy self-image and respect for one's body is an essential part of a person's sexuality. Sometimes a tremendous amount of control is needed to resist the temptations of sex as a hormone-laden teen. Sometimes even as an adult, it takes a whole lot of strength to demand protection in the form of birth control/ STI prevention. And what if one is not supported in the belief that they deserve to have a robust and healthy sense of self-worth? Well, I believe this contributes to the bad judgment we see around sexual activity. I want my children to be able to know, love, and respect their own bodies so they can make decisions that won't put their amazing little bodies needlessly in harm's way as they grow up.

This video is a little treat for you as you finish reading this, especially if you are a woman who has a hard time with this topic.

Video: by Dove, "Amy," 2007
http://www.youtube.com/watch?v=RWNYndqFTR455

You are beautiful and amazing.

Pleasure

To touch can be to give life.

~ Michelangelo

Pleasure: *The simple power of human touch like a hug, that pleasure is more than just "sexual," recognition that any sexual pleasure should be there for both/all parties, not just one person (which at present is usually the male).*

Pleasure is an important component of sexuality that lots of adults recognize. In practice though, it's difficult for other adults to even acknowledge. And for still others, it's even more difficult to fathom pleasure as a component when it comes to our children. Yet we must consider how we gradually introduce this concept to our children, since pleasurable sexuality is the ideal sexuality that they will experience as they grow into adults.

The Healing Power of Touch

There are few pleasures in the world that are still free of financial costs, and by that, I mean things that bring people joy and happiness, broader than carnal pleasure. The first one that to comes to mind, besides the beauty of nature, is a hug. A simple hug is so powerful. Getting a hug from someone when you really need it can feel so good. If you are crying, sometimes a hug can soothe those tears. When you are upset, getting that much-needed hug can evoke tears. Pleasure is physical touch and can develop into physical intimacy, but it represents more than just sexual fulfillment . . . and it is good for all ages.

A good place to begin here is with an overview of attachment theory. Broadly speaking, this is a model some psychologists use to describe the behavior between humans and their interpersonal relationships. More specifically, it attempts to describe our earliest experiences of bonding emotionally and physically with another—usually a primary caregiver—and how that becomes the predictor of future behavior in future relationships. It follows that a secure bond with a parent or other nurturing caregiver leads the way to healthy attachments when one gets older. Conversely, when one does not have a secure attachment, problems develop later on. The *JRank Psychology Encyclopedia* covers the topic under parent-child relationships and writes:

> "The quality of the infant's attachment seems to be predictive of aspects of later development. Youngsters who emerge from infancy with a secure attachment stand a better chance of developing happy, competent relationships with others. The attachment relationship not only forms the emotional basis for the continued development of the parent-child relationship

but can serve as a foundation upon which subsequent social relationships are built."[56]

Physical contact and closeness are important not only for bonding but also for physical, emotional, and psychological health.

Some of you may recall the (controversial) research involving rhesus monkeys conducted in the 1950s. Professor Harry Harlow set out to study love and performed a series of surrogate wire mother experiments with young rhesus monkeys. He removed them from their mother at infancy and instead offered them a wire-and-wood surrogate "mother" either wrapped in cloth or left with the wire exposed. Another control was whether the wire or cloth mother provided nourishment (a bottle) or not. Sometimes a wire mother with a bottle was offered next to a cloth mother without a bottle. Even though none of the "mothers" could embrace the monkey baby, they preferred the cloth wire mother regardless of whether the mother provided the bottle or not. The experiments gave us a glimpse into the importance touch can have even if it is one-sided. Interestingly, when you remember that traditional advice of those days thought it was best to limit or avoid touching children; otherwise, you would spoil them. Some people think that even today, but mainly as it relates to hugging boys.

What is the thinking behind boys being treated differently than girls with regards to affection? I haven't figured this out exactly. In the book *Raising Cain*,[57] Dan Kindlon and Michael Thompson pointed out that "nurturing physical contact with a son grows more awkward and less frequent by around the age eight or nine, but the shift is perhaps most dramatic as he moves into adolescence." It seems it is at that point that parents begin to pull away. Stanford researcher Judy Chu in her book, *When Boys Become Boys*,[58] suggests the impact of culture as opposed to nature is what has an impact on boys' social and emotional skills. The boys are responding to cultural cues about what is masculine and acting this way to reject things that are feminine. All children need compassion, and they would benefit from learning how to demonstrate this to others for their whole lives.

Considering how important touch, comfort, and love is to a child, can you begin to understand the trouble I see us getting into when children aren't able to hug their teachers[59] at school or other caregivers because of a fear of sexually inappropriate touch? Our culture is pretty touch-deprived. It has been the case that a few bad apples have spoiled the whole bunch. Whether from a mother, father, grandparent, or other nurturing caregivers—anyone in the child's trusted circle—a child needs love and affectionate touch, and they are necessary components of healthy development.

How does this extend to helping children develop into healthy sexuality? Dr. Stella Resnick wrote in her book, *The Heart of Desire*:

> "Scientific research tells us that the most profoundly fulfilling intimacies for adults are those that are rooted in the body and involve the same primal needs we were born with [. . .]: empathic touch, eye contact, and intimate kissing. I think of these as the ABCs of a deep intimacy—a primal intimacy, the sine qua non of loving and sensual sex."[60]

Can you imagine how exciting and wonderful our sex lives would be as adults if we all had this all of the time from a trusted partner? Some people have this (and should realize how fortunate they are), while others struggle to find this. Hopefully, our children will not struggle and can feel the amazing warmth and joy out of having these three essential forms of touch: empathic touch, eye contact, and intimate kissing.

Pleasure: More Than Just Sexual Pleasure

Recently a friend shared with me that her son in first grade started to reject her while she was a parent volunteer at his school. This was the first time he had been vocal about not wanting her around. Developmentally, this is a normal thing, as some grade-school kids wish to broaden their social circles. I told her it doesn't mean he is rejecting her or his relationship with her. Quite simply, kids at that age haven't figured out how to multitask their love and attention yet. Sadly, this type of rejection has an impact on parents—but it doesn't have to! If your child does this to you, do not pull away, reject them back, or punish them for it. It's a phase that should pass quickly, provided the adults don't ruminate on the situation.

My children began to reject me when they were about that age as well. I saw this pattern of not wanting to hug mom or dad anymore. I began to point the behavior out to my children when we would see it while spending time around older kids and explained that some kids will act like they don't need or want hugs from their parents. But what I also did was tell my children that as long as they wanted hugs from me, I would be willing to hug them. I also explained that these adolescent years would be challenging because while they're going to want to be a child who can hug mom or dad, they are also going to want to be more independent and grown up. My children also know the Virginia Satir quote, "We need four hugs a day for survival. We need eight hugs a day for maintenance. We need twelve hugs a day for growth." This is the baseline for our daily interactions. Even now as leggy tweens, they ask me often if I can "hold them like a baby" while they sit on my lap. Their smiles and snuggles make it so worthwhile. Yet holding them on my lap when they are over five feet tall, I'm struck by how it was not so long ago that they were tiny babies inside of me.

Hugs happen all the time in my house and for no reason. One analogy we use in our house illustrating the value of hugs, is we compare people to all of the electronic devices in our lives: phones, laptops, tablets, etc. All those items need to be charged, and we plug them into an outlet to do so. We picture ourselves as devices that need to be recharged as well, and hugs are the means of plugging into a power source. We further hypothesize that some people are a trickle charger and others are a rapid charger (and then there are others who drain our batteries instead of filling us up). I hug and squeeze my kids a lot at home and in public, even when their friends are over at our house. A couple of Marcia's friends have voiced to her privately that they wish their moms hugged them as much as I do. Hugs feel good.

This is also where the skills from communication come in. If a person can identify that they *need* a hug, can articulate that they *want* a hug, and has a consenting parent, sibling, friend, or partner to give one then that is wonderful. This is a skill that is transferrable to their adult years. I want my children to associate pleasant, consensual physical contact as pleasurable. It's like developing a muscle memory—one that I want them to associate with positively when they get older.

Touch truly is so much more than sexual pleasure. Dacher Keltner, PhD, professor at the University of California-Berkeley, wrote in his Greater Good Science Center blog, "The science of touch convincingly suggests that we're wired to—we need to—connect with other people on a basic physical level. To deny that is to deprive ourselves of some of life's greatest joys and deepest comforts."[61] And pleasure is both joy and comfort.

Recognition That Any Sexual Pleasure Should Be There for Both/All Parties, Not Just One Person

Our children deserve to learn that pleasure is a necessary component in any sexual activity. The recognition that sexual pleasure should be there for all parties is important when you consider the ramifications of not learning that. Right now, given that we do not acknowledge or teach how pleasure functions in our sexual relationships, our culture and socialization usually dictate that the male gets all the pleasure. In Greek mythology, Tiresias settled an argument between Hera and Zeus on this topic. Tiresias reported that women derive ten times more pleasure from sex than men—he knew this because he lived as a man, then a woman, and again as a man. No wonder women's sexuality and pleasure has been controlled through the ages!

Dr. Justin Lehmiller has written about how crucial touch is to physical intimacy[62] in a successful relationship. Our hands give comfort and convey compassion, and they can also share sexual pleasure. As an adult, do you take the time to learn every spot, every inch of your partner's body? Do you know how and where they like to be touched (keeping in mind that touch doesn't have to be directed to the genitals to be pleasurable)? Is this touch that you share with each other? If not, why not? One of the most powerful tools in a sexologist's toolbox is sensate focus,"[63] an exercise introduced by sex researchers Masters and Johnson. It aims to help individuals learn pleasurable touch for themselves and/or a partner and to communicate that pleasure to their partner. Over time, many relationships experience a decrease in the amount of touch between partners; this leads to resentment, distance, disappointment, and sometimes depression. We want to feel a closeness to our partners, and touch is one of the best ways to be close and intimate.

It is also important to find all of the other things that give you pleasure. What are they? Is it food, exercise, a hobby? How do you find those things, and what do they teach you about you? Kids need this support too. They can use the support to discover the things they enjoy so they can develop a healthy sense of who they are and what they need, want, and desire before they try to find a mate. I believe that doing so will help them respect their body but also feed their soul.

I hear of situations where teens are engaged in sexual activity; sometimes it's not even because they are interested in the sexual behavior itself. There are all sorts of reasons teens might want to have sex: intimacy, status, acceptance, attention, pleasure. Some of these situations may put them more at risk. The double standard that women can't be sexual but men can is not fair either. We live in a society where women aren't supposed to like sex. One such example is that women can't talk about contraception without shame (women who carry condoms have been viewed as sluts, especially by other women).

There are no models for adults to learn from or see what healthy sexuality is supposed to look like. Movies that do attempt to show female pleasure get bad ratings from the MPAA that force the directors to change their depictions or eliminate it altogether. The MPAA's negative attitude toward sexuality and toward female sexuality in particular is exhausting. Rape (which isn't even sex!) gets a pass, as do positive depictions of male sexuality. Sex acts depicting female pleasure? Those make people nervous.[64] Lots of women don't really get to learn on their own or get "training" with a partner who will be attentive and listen because pleasure has not been part of what we learn about sex. Women sometimes don't even get support when they do express how far they want to go, resulting in coercion past their boundaries. Conversely, other women make the "good girl" declaration that "I'm not going to sleep with you tonight" (and then they do).

I am deeply concerned about how young adults use sex. I feel many teens get started with sexual behaviors because no one will help them process or break down the feelings and desires they have. They are denied an authentic exploration and seem to act out in ways that allow them to do so without any responsibility (and that puts them in situations where they may need to assume a tremendous amount of responsibility with becoming a parent or dealing with potential health issues). If we adults could move to a broader understanding of human sexuality, take a position of tolerance around the concept of our children as sexual beings and understand how our tolerance can help them grow in healthy ways in their attitudes about sexuality, then maybe we can begin to acknowledge the importance of pleasure in their education about sexuality.

My Child Skipped the "Where Did I Come From" Question

My daughters knew I studied sex at school. Actually, if you would have heard Marcia tell it, she said her mom is "studying people's bodies," which at the time was age appropriate.

Anyway, I have many "school supplies" in my home, and because my focus is on helping parents talk with their children about sex, I have many European children's books. Most of these cover simple reproductive biology but also condoms, abortion, and masturbation. On the other hand, American books don't talk about much besides reproductive biology and anatomy/physiology, let alone pleasure or fantasy as they relate to human sexuality for adults, teens, or children. So, you can imagine my surprise when one day, my eight-year-old came to me and asked, "How do you have sex and not get pregnant?"

Not only did she skip the dreaded, "Mom, where did I come from?" (she didn't ask the typical question because we already went through the topics of pregnancy and childbirth at length), but she went straight for the throat. Not to mention, she asked the question in a way that prevented me from answering, "Don't have it."

My basic approach to this topic is to answer as best I can in one sentence. I told her that women can get a pill from their doctor that prevents pregnancy, but it doesn't protect against sexually transmitted infections. She asked what those are, and I explained that they were sicknesses a person may or may not even know they have that can make people contagious, sick, and/or even die. She asked, "What about the man? Does he have to take a pill?" I told her about condoms and how they protect us from pregnancy and STIs. She asked how, and I told her it was like a special sock for a penis that protects both people during sexual intercourse. She giggled a bit and wandered away to play.

This interaction was short, sweet, and to the point and that was all she wanted to know. Of course, there are lots of possible answers I could have given her, but I wanted to be as brief, accurate, and understandable as possible. This keeps her from being overwhelmed, and she can stop me whenever she wants.

I realized two things afterward.

1. I didn't start with asking her what she knew already. Now, I see that as an opportunity for every parent to gauge how much the child does already know and redirect any misinformation (which is rampant!).

2. My answer was very hetero-centric (having heterosexual sexual behavior as the center or focus). I hoped for another

opportunity to fix that.

Then She Asked Again

Months later, my daughter asked me about sex again. She asked me if there were more ways to have sex and not get pregnant. I was bummed after I gave my answer to her last question because my answer was very hetero-centric, simply meaning defining sex as only penile-vaginal (P/V) intercourse.

I'm building up to my answer: not many people like to talk about "this." "This" is highly controversial stuff. The "this" I'm referring to is masturbation. Some call it self-love or self-pleasuring, along with other more jokey or silly names, depending upon your gender.

Dr. Jocelyn Elders was forced to resign her post as US Surgeon General in December 1994 after suggesting masturbation to be taught in sex ed! She was asked at a World AIDS Day conference if she would consider promoting masturbation as a means of preventing young people from engaging in riskier forms of sexual activity. Elder, as quoted in *U.S. News and World Report* responded, "With regard to masturbation, I think that it is something that is a part of human sexuality and a part of something that should perhaps be taught."[65] Dr. Elders is a very wise woman, yet her sensible position caused people to freak out.

Genital self-stimulation is very natural; some babies in their first year of life explore their bodies, and this behavior has been observed in utero as well. But it is also important to remember that we as adults tend to sexualize things that a child does not see as sexual, and a child's self-stimulating behavior is not "masturbation" like an adult. I think this fact is an important piece to remember: when a child overhears that two people are sleeping together, they picture two people snuggling in the same bed (something they probably like to do with a parent or caregiver), whereas an adult understands "sleeping together" to mean sex. This is sexualization, making something sexual.

Back to my answer to Marcia's question:

Me: "I'm so happy you asked. I realized last time you asked me I forgot THE very best way. You are not going to get pregnant, and you are not going to get any sexually transmitted infections! It's called masturbation."

Her: "What's that?"

Me: "It's when you touch your private parts."

Her: "Do YOU do that?"

*Me: (Ugh. I did NOT expect the line of questioning to go this way. Did I REALLY say I was going to try to be up-front and honest about this stuff?) *blushing* "Weelll, yeeeaaahh."*

Her: "You do?!" (incredulous)

Me: "Yeah, but I didn't until I was older, mainly because Grandma told me only girls who are dirty, nasty, or naughty do that. As I got older, I realized that was a bunch of nonsense."

Her: (grinning) "Really?"

Me: "There are all kinds of things people say about masturbation that simply aren't true. But it's your body. It belongs to you. I'm okay with you touching your parts. But keep your hands clean. And please keep it private, say when you are alone in your room or in the bathroom. It's not something you do in public." (That last sentence said with emphasis to lighten the mood.)

Marcia , giggling, fell into the folded clothes on the bed. We snuggled and laughed together, big smiles on our faces.

Masturbation has many benefits. It improves immune function, relieves menstrual cramps, and it is the safest kind of sex—meaning it is risk-free, no chance for pregnancy or STIs. Masturbation also helps a person know his or her own body better and learn what feels good. Some parents prefer their teens release the sexual tension alone than feel pressure to have P/V sex. All of this reminds me of my favorite line in an episode of the TV show *Weeds* about masturbation.[66] Uncle Andy says, *"Practice makes perfect, so work on your control now while you are a solo artist and you'll be playing some long happy duets in the future."*

As for what Grandma said, some would say masturbation IS dirty and nasty . . . but in the GOOD way.

Self-Love and Masturbation

I have a confession to make. Blogging about masturbation was so incredibly difficult for me. It really made me wonder what my mom said to me about masturbation all those years ago. I think it had a pretty significant impact on the sexuality of my young adult life. I've long thought that my interest in the field of psychology, women's studies, and human sexuality has a lot to do with my very sexually repressed Catholic upbringing. Since I wrote that blog, I went through a class about how to help pre-orgasmic women (defined as women who have not yet had an orgasm). In it, I unraveled my own first memory of my first orgasm. I'm forty-two years old now, and it took thirty years to recall it.

So, it raises a question for me: Why do some parents shame their children about behaviors that feel good and that don't harm the child? Besides the obvious religious abuse around the topic, what is wrong with it? I'll note here that when I say religious abuse, I'm using the same definition as listed on Wikipedia: "abuse administered under the guise of religion, including harassment or humiliation, possibly resulting in psychological trauma."

Well-meaning instances of such abuse are often motivated by genuine concern that the targeted person will come to physical or spiritual harm should they engage in a certain behavior or question their beliefs. The perpetrator then uses exaggerated, distorted, or even false versions of their teachings or their position of authority to instill intense fear and/or shame so that the victim will comply.

Typically, lots of parents of girls either don't talk about masturbation or they tell their daughters, "Don't do it." Whereas parents of boys tend to adopt a sort of "don't ask, don't tell" attitude on the subject. Unless it comes up, then they might say, "boys will be boys," and may look the other way. You as the parent are entitled to have your own views and opinions on this topic. Obviously. If you do not believe it's okay to masturbate and wish to share that with your children, that's your right as the parent. You should share that as your belief/values (religious or otherwise), but make sure to give accurate, factual information about masturbation as well. No, hair will NOT grow on your palms. No, you will NOT go blind. No, it won't hurt you. Marcia caught me off guard when she asked me if I masturbated (I should have seen that coming . . .).

Bottom line, parents who shame their children around masturbation are really messing with their children's heads. If parents tell their children things that are not true about masturbation, it creates a huge amount of anxiety and cognitive dissonance (a discomfort caused by holding conflicting ideas simultaneously) in the children. I understand, it isn't anything parents want to talk about with their children; however, it goes right along with teaching them about the changes that occur in their bodies as they grow. I can't imagine how freaked out I would be if I was a boy and woke up after a wet dream but had no idea if that was normal. It's an uncomfortable conversation, but it's totally okay to acknowledge such. If it fits for you, you can say, "My parent(s) didn't talk to me about this, and I kind of wish they did. I'm nervous now talking to you about this, but I want to be here for you because there's a lot of information out there and not all of it is good. I want you to have the correct answers. If I don't know the answer, I'll go find out and get back to you."

So, how can something that feels so good really be so wrong? Masturbation is self-love. It is instructional and helps an individual understand the functioning of their body. It helps relieve menstrual cramps in women. It improves one's mood. It relieves stress. Most importantly, the concern for most parents is that it allows a person to be sexual without engaging another person, or risk contracting STIs, or risk getting pregnant.

Can someone tell me, what ARE the drawbacks again?

Naughty Christmas Cookies? Is That Sacrilege?

This year was the first year in a long time that I made and decorated sugar cookies for the holidays with my girls. I used to bake a ton but pretty much gave up after needing to go gluten-free; this year I decided to give gluten-free baking a go. My daughters looked forward to rolling out the dough, cutting out the shapes, and frosting, etc. We made the dough from scratch and dug out of storage all the standard shapes: mittens, bells, stars, and gingerbread men. And we had tons of frosting colors.

After the dough was ready, we started with cutting out the cookies. The girls wanted to differentiate the "people" cookies somehow, and since I didn't have a gingerbread woman shape, we made a teeny-tiny little indentation with the side of the spatula for a vulva on one of the cookies. The girls giggled with laughter at the simplicity of the solution and wholeheartedly agreed that a cookie doesn't need a skirt to be a woman.

The time came for baking. The girls could hardly wait for the cookies to get out of the oven, let alone to cool on the rack. But finally, once the yummy goods were cooled, the fun of frosting began. I needed to run out to get something for dinner, so a sitter stayed with them for this part. I returned to see the typical shapes got decorated with a more traditional style, but when it came time to decorate the people, it got a little creative! The girls figured out that you could layer the frosting for "breasts," so some cookie people had extra frosting mounds on them. Cindy put a little extra frosting on the crotch of one (to indicate a bulge for a penis). Cindy also made a cookie that was dressed like Redfoo from LMFAO's video "I'm Sexy and I Know It" complete with hair (black frosting) under his arms. My friend who came over while this production was underway noted that this style of cookie decorating was what he and friends did when they were teens, only privately out of the sight of adults.

Of course, as expected, after a few silly cookies, the novelty wore off and they resumed the more traditional cookie decorating.

I know it is not typical in most households to allow children to be silly in this way—I'm sure my own mother would have strong words with me if she hears about this—but we were having so much fun together. Perhaps this was how you wished you could have made cookies when you were growing up? Perhaps you did . . . are you any worse for the wear? Like I said, the silliness was short-lived and the bottom line is we had a ball. I'm sure this will be a lasting positive memory for them as it will be for me.

There is so much lightness and fun to be had around this topic, and I truly believe making this difficult topic easy now will make the tougher conversations that will come later easier.

Are Men God's Gift to Women? No, the Clitoris Is

Does anyone else find it odd that there is little to no discussion of the role of the clitoris in sex education in general? Does anyone (besides my sex educator friends and colleagues) know the extended physiology of the clitoral structure?

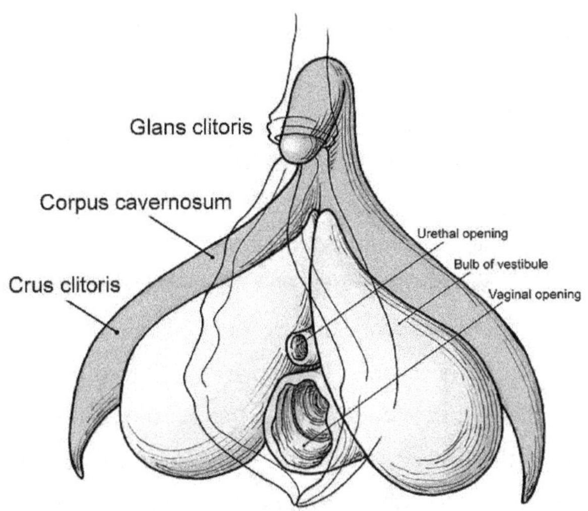

Internal clitoral structure[67]

This vast structure is just under the surface of the vulva.

Why is this? Do you know how utterly amazing the clitoris is?

There certainly is plenty of information on the penis. And most teenage boys know how it works from their own "hands-on" experience. Many teenage girls don't often have that luxury of self-knowledge and awareness that boys do.

One of my favorite authors, Susie Bright, wrote a book called *Mommy's Little Girl: On Sex, Motherhood, Porn and Cherry Pie.*[68] In it she wrote:

> *"The girls know that boys urinate through their penis–and also when they are older, are able to 'have sex' with the same piece of equipment, but what do girls 'have sex' with? Most girls don't know. They know that boys get off with these penises of theirs; but they're not sure whether they have something that would make them feel the same way [. . .] These girls are smart and inquisitive, [. . .] but they are also deliberately kept ignorant of their intrinsic female anatomy to the point of not even knowing the names of anything below the waist."*

So, in those first sexual heterosexual experiences, even if both are virgins, the male often knows part of what is "supposed" to happen in those first encounters because he knows how his plumbing works. The female? Not so much. Plus, most of the education these children get is information from porn and/or peers with bravado. Add to that, abstinence-only before marriage sex education surely isn't telling them what to do or how to protect themselves "because abstinence is the absolute safest way to avoid STIs and pregnancy." Safest yes, but not realistic. If females aren't aware that things are supposed to feel good, chances are they will engage in this behavior because others want it, not because they understand what is happening. Ask a girl who has had sex for the first time about the experience and often she will tell you how she looked, not how she felt. What is wrong with this?!

So many people I talk to who work with kids between the ages nine to fourteen tell me stories that break my heart, especially the stories of how girls are unaware of how sex relates to them. As pointed out above, these young girls know some of the reproductive biology of sex, the mechanics: a man ejaculates, and to some of them that equals "sex." But what is the woman's sexual response cycle and what is the function of the clitoris and its role in sex? Without this information, everything young women learn about sex happens outside of them and their bodies, and that it's something women do for someone else, mostly because they have not yet learned or been told that it's about pleasure (gasp!).

The Good Men Project published a blog, *"Because It Feels Good: The Starting Point for Talking to Children About Sex"*:

> *"When we tell girls that sex is something people do when they love each other, it sets them up to believe that sex is sacrificial. So, when Jassie falls in love with Bobby, and Bobby pushes for intercourse, she's conditioned to focus on 'giving it up' for him rather than on thinking about what feels good for her. The more she's taught that her pleasure matters, the less likely she'll be coerced into going farther than her body is ready to go. 'It's supposed to feel good,' she may remember, 'and right now, being rushed and pawed doesn't feel good. So, I want to stop.' Centering pleasure gives young women a power that centering love doesn't."*[69]

There are plenty of stories [urban myth/moral panic?] about young teens and their so-called Rainbow Parties. No wonder some of these teenage girls have claimed their sexual "power" by giving blow jobs to their male peers. But honestly! What. Do. These.

Girls. Get. Out. Of. It? I'm less shocked by them performing oral sex and more shocked by the fact that I'm not so sure if they are aware of the reasons for their behavior or in touch with how they feel about what they are doing.

Let me ask you this: Do you know that the sole function of the female clitoris is for pleasure? Read that again. The sole function of the female clitoris is for pleasure. It is the only part of the body that has that honorable distinction. Conservatives should note: God loves us women enough to give us this amazing clitoris that has NO other function than for pleasure! We must teach or simply tell each other (including men) that there is supposed to be a connection between the arousal we sense in our minds and the physical response we feel between our legs. Many times, this mind-body connection has been severed through shaming, religious abuse, or guilt. There is no need for that anymore.

More and more women are standing up and asking for what they want in their sexual relationships. And the clitoris deserves some attention. We owe it to the young women who will come after us (pun intended?).

Fantasy

In every [hu]man, a child is hidden that wants to play.

~ Friedrich Nietzsche

Fantasy: *It's important to encourage and maintain a childlike curiosity and focus; what we learn about sex, outside of formal education, is fantasy; it's okay to have fantasies, and they don't all have to be acted upon or fulfilled.*

The toughest of the five building blocks is fantasy. Why is this important for our kids, and how do we talk about it? Most adults don't admit their own fantasies to a partner and lots more don't talk about the subject at all. Again, the understanding of the importance of fantasy comes once you consider the potential benefits. Like the other building blocks, we can gradually develop and reinforce this through their lives to adulthood. There may even be some knowledge in here you can use immediately to undo some of the more harmful ideas you have learned that have impacted your experiences.

Childlike Curiosity and Focus

Have you ever watched children when they are in their own fantasy world? They are completely enthralled and cannot be interrupted. Nothing can stop them from the focus they have on the story or the task at hand. They are not as concerned with appearance, continuity, or reality. They play and get enjoyment from it. Play is work for them. In kindergarten, it's okay to play. When we are young, we create characters and story lines, do role plays, invent games, and pretend, all while using our imagination. When does this end? Somewhere along the line, we are told to stop daydreaming. Grow up. Live in the real world. Where does fantasy end for kids who identify as female? For many, it ends with dolls. Fortunately, some games cross genders that girls play as well. Some teens find age-appropriate fantasy in which to participate: paintball and simulation/role play video games like *Minecraft*, *World of Warcraft,* and *Halo*. We shouldn't be telling our children which toys to play with as long as it engages their imagination. For all of this fantasy, there is a proper time and place just like there is for masturbation.

Now, have you ever watched an adult playing with a child? Most adults don't allow themselves to play the same way—they're absorbed with the task at hand; some of them have cell phones or other distractions within arm's reach. Many adults discount child-like tasks or brush it off as "child's play." But we should play like children more often. Can you imagine how much more pleasurable our adult sexual interactions would be if we, along with our partners, were completely immersed in what we were doing? Even alone, fantasy can be beneficial. In *The Hite Report*,[70] originally published in 1976, over 3,000 women from all over the country answered a variety of questions about female sexuality. Many women talked about how they incorporate fantasy into their masturbation practices. This type of play enables us to learn about what we like, how we like it, and how our bodies work. Men and boys get this practice in their masturbation patterns, but this is often overlooked for women.

It's okay to fantasize. And it's important to acknowledge that not all fantasies need to be acted out or fulfilled. There are plenty of adults who cannot admit and don't talk about their fantasies with other adults, certainly not their partners. Some fear judgment or embarrassment, others are afraid of how someone else might react, others don't want to hurt the feelings of their partners or they feel their fantasies might be too strange. Ideally, we create an environment that doesn't squash fantasy. Ideally, we should help our children balance fantasy and reality. As parents, our position with our children can be nonjudgmental, modeling that it is okay to fantasize, and in effect opening the door for their future relationships to be nonjudgmental.

What we learn about sex, outside of formal education, is fantasy.

Psychologist Bernie Zilbergeld, author of *The New Male Sexuality*, wrote:

> "Whether we know it or not, whether it's intended or not, sex education goes on all the time, from the day we're born until the day we die, with an especially heavy dose coming at puberty. Long before we are exposed to the realities of sex, our heads are filled with all sorts of nonsense. Every time we tell or listen to a sexual joke, watch a movie that depicts sexuality explicitly or implicitly, read a novel or see a television program that involves sex or adult relationships–at all these

times and many others, either we learn something about sex or, more likely, something we already believe is reinforced and strengthened."[71]

It's essential to understand that aside from any real education about sexuality, most of the messages we receive about sex and sexuality are fantasy. Because we don't have good sex education, we follow and believe this model of sex. When we don't have real or accurate information about sex, then we only have the fantasies (porn, romance novels, and media) to compare ourselves to. Again, from *The New Male Sexuality: The Fantasy Model of Sex*:

Myth 1: We're liberated folks who are very comfortable with sex.

Myth 2: A real man isn't into sissy stuff like feelings and communicating.

Myth 3: All touching is sexual or should lead to sex.

Myth 4: A man is always interested in and always ready for sex.

Myth 5: A real man performs in sex.

Myth 6: Sex is centered on a hard penis and what's done with it.

Myth 7: If your penis isn't up to snuff, we have a pill that will take care of everything.

Myth 8: Sex equals intercourse.

Myth 9: A man should make the earth move for his partner, or at the very least knock her socks off.

Myth 10: Good sex is spontaneous, with no planning and no talking.[72]

Porn is not keeping people sexually dumb; porn is just entertainment and depicts fantasy, not real life. We are keeping each other sexually dumb—by using shame, judgment, guilt, and disgust. How? This happens when someone tells us what they are interested in and we react with any response other than just "listening" to what they like. No turned-up noses. No sneers. We should be listening to each other with nothing but curiosity. Ask any sexologist or person who deals with clients around human sexuality will tell you the most common concern people want to know is if they are "normal." Lots of times, once you talk about something and break it down, the power it once had disappears.

Adults consume different media, they build different models that sometimes aren't compatible, and then conflicts and disappointments arise. The messaging is that most boys want to have sex with anyone who will have it with them. Conversely, girls are told they shouldn't want sex, yet many do. They are just less likely to go about it the same way boys do. It distills down to one fact: unless we get comprehensive sexuality education, all we have is the above fantasy model and that does nothing but hurt those who don't know better.

It's okay to have fantasies and they don't all have to be acted upon or fulfilled.

There are lots of fantasies out there. Millions. Billions even.[73] The important thing to note is that it is okay not to act out a fantasy. Lots of times it doesn't play out the way one wishes. Then that fantasy risks being ruined and/or losing its allure. That's okay, and sometimes just talking about them can be satisfying.

For teenagers and young adults, I see a big difference between watching adult video/porn and reading erotica. *Fifty Shades of Grey*[74] is a recent example of popular "fantasy" fiction that opened a lot of minds to a fantasy they maybe hadn't considered before. In terms of content, I don't think that series was any worse than the porn available to them on the internet. However, *Fifty Shades of Grey* is not the best source of information on proper BDSM practices (it's really bad, actually). Think of this: have you ever picked up a book that you just couldn't get interested in? You don't end up reading it, do you? But turn on an adult video and it is so much tougher to turn away. It's like watching a train wreck. Video leaves nothing to the imagination. I think it's okay for children/teens/adults to have information that sex should be about pleasure.

Here again, without good comprehensive sex education, this book and other materials and videos of this genre are all our kids get about sex, and *it's all someone else's fantasy*; it's not real. This is not helpful to them. Make sure you have a conversation with your kids if they check it out. Tell them that there are a bunch of misconceptions about BDSM and healthy relationships in general in the books and start a discussion. You likely won't get into too much about the sex, but the bits about healthy relationships will benefit them in the long run. Tell them that if they have any questions to come to you and together you'll do your best to explain things.

Teaching abstinence is fine, yet you must know it does not get the desired results. Abstinence-only education is riddled with untruths and misleading information.[75] A comprehensive review article from the 2006 *Journal of Adolescent Health*,[76] "Abstinence and Abstinence-Only Education: A Review of US Policies and Programs," says:

> "Although abstinence until marriage is the goal of many abstinence policies and programs, few Americans wait until marriage to initiate sexual intercourse. Most Americans initiate sexual intercourse during their adolescent years. Recent data indicates that the median age at first intercourse for women was 17.4 years, whereas the median age at first marriage was 25.3 years."[77]

What do you think the results are going to be when you realize that's roughly eight years of raging hormones and desires? Some are going to experiment. This happened to Sarah Palin's seventeen-year-old daughter in 2008 and to Louisiana Senator Bill Cassidy's seventeen-year-old daughter in 2013—just two of the higher-profile instances of proselytizing while wearing blinders. You can hope that your teen isn't one of them. Or, instead of telling them not to do anything, let them know they have some pregnancy and STI-proof outlets: masturbation and fantasy.

Make sure you are giving real information and you are talking to your children about your values. If you have teenagers, maybe you can include some personal experience and why you feel the way you do. Think of it this way: what would you say to the sixteen-year-old you knowing what you know now? What would you want to know if you were sixteen about sex? Fantasy is okay. Reading something doesn't necessarily mean they're going to act on it. Do you go out and do everything you read? There's no such thing as bad thoughts, only bad actions. Make sure you let your child know that a lot of sexual information out there is fantasy, just like the porn they see freely on the internet.

If your teen talked to you about *Fifty Shades of Grey* or other adult materials they have come across, it is a good sign they are comfortable talking to you. I think erotica is the lesser of two evils. Remember your reaction to a book that doesn't hold your interest? I usually put a book down that bores me. The same will hold true for your kids. Books are easy to put down if you don't "get it." Some teens have sex earlier, some have it later. Many parents deny their own kids' involvement in anything sexual, some even balk at the notion that their adolescent child should learn anything about sexuality in seventh grade. The facts show that a small percentage (7.9 percent) of kids are already engaging with others sexually by age fourteen,[78] the majority of those under age twelve are nonconsensual. Those parents that turn a blind eye to their teenager's desires (and maybe even to their own or to their partner's desires?) are denying the power of fantasy. Teens who initiate sex at young ages take longer to initiate contraceptive use. Only 52 percent of those starting to have sex at twelve or younger use contraception during the first month of sex, and figures are relatively low for thirteen- and fourteen-year-olds as well.[79] Those parents who do talk openly about sex have a better chance of their children using contraception than kids whose parents avoid the topic[80] to "protect their innocence."

It's the same issue I have with kids watching videos when they're young. One example that jumps out at me: watching the 1991 Disney movie version of *Beauty and the Beast*[81] is a different experience than it would be if they read it. There are all kinds of fantasy messages in this movie. Some of the scenes normalize behaviors that domestic violence treatment programs say are problematic to healthy loving relationships (Gaston tosses a chair aside while advancing menacingly toward Belle in her cottage; Beast controls where Belle goes; she is not allowed to go outside the castle; Belle is kept from seeing her father; Beast yells at Belle and informs her that she is NOT allowed into a certain part of the castle, etc.). And we wonder why women don't see the signs of domestic abuse earlier!

Getting back to healthy fantasy, reading a book without images encourages one to use their imagination, and the mind can create the story for the individual. Porn/adult video is also terrible for not leaving anything to the imagination. Sex and relationship expert, Reid Mihalko, once said, "Trying to learn how to be a better lover from watching most mainstream porn is like trying to learn how to drive from watching *The Fast and The Furious*."[82] It doesn't work that way. Children and adults deserve a better education than what they get right now, which is so much fantasy and not enough real information.

#Porn

Speaking of porn (a.k.a. adult video), parents have a range of reactions to their children's access to porn or adult video on the internet. What is the long-term effect of this exposure? A comprehensive report came out of Middlesex University London[83] in May 2013 saying the findings are inconclusive as to the effects of porn on the sexual development of children and teens. So why do they go looking for it? One thing does seem clear: kids are turning to porn because they don't like the sex education they are getting, and they expect porn to teach them.

They're not alone: I know plenty of adults who use it for "education" as well. So, what has affected the sexual development of children and teens the most? In my opinion, it's the *lack* of open, honest, accurate sex education, including teaching about concepts not typically thought of when dealing with genitals: communication, consent, respect, pleasure, and fantasy.

People are very afraid of what porn exposure could mean to their children. You can be the most conscientious parent—blocking all your computers' browsers, adding all the filters, making everything password-protected, locking everything down, but it won't do what you hope. I'm sorry to burst your bubble. If kids really want to find it, they will find ways to get around your roadblocks. All it takes is going to a friends' house whose computer/smartphone/tablet is not locked down to find what they seek. When I was a kid and I really wanted to know something, I found ways to get around the blocks. They are going to get it elsewhere. You must be brave and tackle the topic head-on. What did I tell my two girls? Most important: **there are things you can't "unsee" out there.** I sat my kids down and explained that to them that Google is not a friend for finding information about sex. You don't know what you're going to get in a search. Then, once you see something, you can't easily forget it or wipe it clean from your memory. I find this to be true for video more than pictures or images. Give your child a non-porn example of your own where you saw something that stuck with you and is an image burned into your brain. For me, it's the scene in the movie *Alien* where the alien jumps out of the guy's stomach; I wish I could unsee that. Each of my kids can relate to this because they too can recall movie moments that bother them. Their examples may be tame comparatively speaking, but that's not important. What's important is they can understand.

Bringing this back to porn, it is important to tell them that what they see in porn is someone else's fantasy, and it's not real; porn is not always an accurate depiction of what people do nor how they think about sex. Porn is not something one should view as a "how-to" or "how it should be" guide. It is edited for flow, and there are lots of things that happen during filming that you don't see in the video. There will also be things in porn that will disturb their young minds because they won't understand what the actors are doing or how to process the images they see on the screen. You can share with your kids that watching porn is not a good way to get an education about sex.

Bottom line, regardless of whether it is about porn or sex in general, sheltering your children is not helpful to them. You are not with them all the time, and many factors (their peers, TV, movies, or things they Google on their devices) will have a greater amount of influence the older they get. We can be most successful as parents to give our children the tools and information they need to succeed in life. Teaching about sexuality is no different. If you would prefer that your child gets the correct information about sex, then sexuality needs to be discussed, incorporating your own values and morals about the topic and accurate information needs to be shared by you. If not, someone else will do it for you.

Let's think this through given that 95 percent of people have sex before marriage,[84] it seems those people who endorse or teach an abstinence-only-before marriage-based curriculum must be unwilling to admit that abstinence-only-before-marriage sex education does not work. 95 percent! To me, this means we should take every opportunity we have to make sure our kids have good information to be able to make good choices on their own, if and when it should come to that. In the meantime, for those who want to continue to use the "abstinence-only" curriculums, I encourage you to reconsider the benefits of a more comprehensive approach. I agree that abstinence is the best way to avoid getting pregnant, but one can also teach the many ways to be sexual (read: without having actual penetrative sex). Comprehensive sexual education includes teaching about the benefits of abstinence, of course. I simply want to make it clear that abstinence cannot be the only choice given 95 percent of people have sex before marriage.

What if your children are in a school district that doesn't cover sexual education adequately or at all? This puts the responsibility of sex education all on you, the parent. Are you ready for that? Alongside parents doing their best to share their own important values and morals as well as discussions around sex and sexuality, having an expert available to be a resource to help parents answer some of the more challenging questions is great. Personally, I would have a very difficult time answering questions about statistics without needing to go to Khan Academy to watch a video for it. Instead of trying to get answers to thousands of possible questions you might not know the answers to, I have included a list of some of my favorite "experts" to whom you can reach out (as well as me). Some of these experts also have special areas of expertise and can answer many questions in their specialty within this broad field of human sexual behavior. Some may be resources you can turn to for your own sex education needs. These are all in the Appendix at the end of the book.

Think back to when you were young. How was sexual education handled for you? Did you wish you had more information? Teach your children as you wish someone had taught you. If you're one of the lucky ones who had a parent tell you what was what, then follow their lead. If no one taught you or you had poor information, do you wish your child gets this same treatment? What happens if we don't talk to our children and leave it to the kids to figure sex out on their own? I don't want someone else to teach them the values of my family, and when it comes time and my children ask me about my experiences, I will try my best to tell them. And I certainly will make sure they know about the items that make up the foundation for a healthy sexuality, namely communication, consent, respect, pleasure, and fantasy.

Porn and Realism

I received a comment from a dad who had a question about porn and the absence of realism. He wrote:

> *"I am the father of three boys, ages sixteen, fifteen, and ten. The older two especially are filled with the usual crap that comes from middle school and high school boyland. The only thing I have problems dealing with them in the area of sexuality (I hope) is realism. The ease of access to porn seems to set up bizarre expectations. I have never seen in person a man with a penis the size of a loaf of bread or a woman who orgasms from performing fellatio.*
>
> *Part of the problem is that I am their fat old dad who obviously can have no idea what I am talking about. How can I help them learn about the realities of sex?"*

My response was this:

Spoiler Alert

> *"I'll say this up front, if you want to continue living in the fantasy that the porn world is the same as the real world, do not read on. Also, I am not anti-porn; I watch porn from time to time myself. I also know some amazing people in the adult industry like Jessica drake and Tristan Taormino who create entertainment that is a form of erotic education; not all porn is bad porn. Like wine, some of what you can find out there is good, others are not so good.*
>
> *I think as their dad you may have an easier go of this conversation with these boys than their mom or another woman in their life would. (Easier, but no less important. I do think a woman's perspective on this is crucial too). What you said is absolutely real and an excellent thing to point out. I want to invite you to watch*

the following clip by Cindy Gallop (founder of MakeLoveNotPorn.com) at TED2009 talk in Long Beach, CA.[85] *You are truly not alone in your concerns . . .*

Ms. Gallop's website touches on some of the myths of porn and attempts to balance them with reality. Bottom line: some people like those things, some people don't. And that's okay. I'm sure you know this already, but what your sons won't realize is what you see in porn, for the most part, is only one view . . . and that is targeted toward men only. And heterosexual men at that.

There is very little in adult movies that replicates real-life sex—just like movies that are based on fantasy. Have you and your sons ever watched a sci-fi movie and commented on how cool the special effects were? Well, adult movies have special effects too, in a sense. Adult films are shot over a period of time; the guy goes soft, they pause filming to get things going again, resume shooting, and edit together for flow. That means that the rock hard hard-on the guy sports in the video is actually a variety of scenes spliced together to make it look like he was hard for the entire sexual act. And sometimes the moaning that you hear in the videos doesn't match the mouths! That's added later for those who get turned on by auditory stimulation.

I recently watched The Wizard of Oz *with my girls again, and I pointed out the scene where the scarecrow is still up on his post. You can just barely see the fishing line above him as he talks and moves. I pointed this out to my girls and now—while film buffs think I might've ruined the movie for my girls by telling them it was there—my girls mention it every time we watch this movie. I understand digital film editing is much more advanced than it was back in the day, but that's also how porn is sometimes able to 'trick' you into thinking what you see is what you get.*

Even regular movies have all kinds of unrealistic depictions in them; not all of them are sex-related, and that might also be an easy way to ease into a conversation about sex (Don't get me started on all of the messed up impressions your average RomCom Hollywood happy ending has on little girls . . .). Wild Things *is rated R but has a pool scene between* Neve Campbell *and* Denise Richards *that I think every male over age twenty has seen. It also perpetuates the male fantasy that all women are into other women, which comes from porn and is, by the way, not true.*

So, while I've talked about some of the things in porn that aren't real, I'll shift now to having this conversation. If you and your children are relatively open about sex, a straightforward, "How do you feel about such-and-such?" would probably do the trick. You could even go with a different direct approach and say something like, "I know this may be coming out of left field, but I'm concerned about the messages you are getting about sex, sexual behaviors, and what's real or normal from the stuff that's out there. I may be an old guy now, but I was young once too and have probably seen a lot more than you think," or "I want you to know I am here for you whenever you want to talk guy talk because I know when I was your age it was confusing for me. Given the messages I see on YouTube, TV, movies, and magazines, etc. today, I can imagine it's confusing to you too," or whatever honest approach feels right for you.

I'm not sure how comfortable you would be approaching this topic much like the father in this quote does. It is direct, but I enjoy the lecture, in particular. This is from a book by Judith Levine called

Harmful to Minors: The Perils of Protecting Children from Sex:[86]

> *Craig Long, a father I met in Chicago, had carried on a frank and continual conversation with his son, Henry, about sex since earliest childhood. Then, on his eleventh birthday, the boy asked shyly for a* Playboy *magazine. After discussing the matter with Henry's mother, Craig gave him the magazine, accompanied by a small lecture. "I told him real women don't look like the models in* Playboy*, and they're generally not splayed out for immediate consumption." After a few weeks, Craig checked in with his son. Had he been looking at the magazine? "Hmm, not so much." Was he enjoying it? "Hmm, not so much." Why not? "I don't know, Dad," the boy finally said. "I guess I'm too young for this stuff."*[87]

If you want to approach porn and realism more slowly, you could hint at it any number of ways: perhaps send your son a link to a story involving some aspect of whatever the topic is and say you wanted to ask him what he thinks about it. There are plenty of YouTube links that go viral in a matter of days that might offer an opportunity to talk.

In terms of some other approaches to talking that don't involve porn, there is plenty to discuss about current movie themes as well. I don't know what movies you allow your boys to see, but maybe you could suggest that you watch some movie together that raises some interesting topics to discuss. Take the new release Hall Pass *(rated R). If the trailer is any indication (Hall Pass, n.: A week off from marriage to do whatever you want without consequences), then it's going to raise discussions for lots of couples. If your boys are dating, this movie may raise questions for them about marriage and/or long-term commitments. Be there for them but make sure when you discuss it to give them facts and point out what your own values are around the topic.*

There are opportunities everywhere to discuss this topic. Next time you see something together, like a billboard or an ad, ask them what they think. If there is a subtle joke of some sort, ask them if they get it. If YOU don't get it, ask them. Chances are they may have been "enlightened" by a peer at some point.

Finding time to have these discussions can be tricky. I'm not sure if you are able to have these one-on-one conversations or if your opportunities are more for the four of you together. Be aware to do this at a time when you have no other agenda. If you are able to do personal chats, then you could start laying the foundation for starting these talks by going out for a burger or someplace he likes away from his brothers and other distractions—just the two of you—to talk once in a while but be sure to schedule them regularly.

When you do talk, give facts but also talk about your own experiences and values. Talk about the situations where you made mistakes and what you learned from the experience. Try to keep it relevant to what they are experiencing at this age (more can come later). Talk about how and why you made the decisions you did about sex. Own it. Talk about what your parents told you when you were your sons' ages. It's even valuable to say what your parents didn't say and what that meant to you too. Your older boys are presumably mature enough to hear some of this at this time. In general, I think children are able to understand a lot more information than we give them credit.

Be aware too that he may not be ready to talk about anything the first time out. He may want to make sure it's safe telling you or asking you something, especially if this is all new for you guys. Try to gauge your son's interest in talking about these things. Once you two are talking, ask him what he already knows. That's also a good way to correct any misinformation. But be ready to listen—really listen—and don't be surprised if you get a bit shocked by what they have to say. Remember to breathe.

There's a lot here. If I had one thing to say about having these conversations with your sons, it would be to reassure you that you have a lot more expertise to share then you are probably willing to admit. Just by virtue of your own life experiences, you do know what's real and what isn't, and that will be of immense value to them as well. But the fact that you are asking these questions tells me that you love your boys and you want them to have realistic views about sex and ultimately have a healthy adult sex life as well. Hang in there!

There Are Some Things You Can't "Unsee"

Children's curiosity is okay. As they grow, it's important to mindfully attend to what things they are interested in and then, as their parent, guide them as best you can. Here are a couple of examples:

Example 1

Around the time my friend's daughter, Shelly, was nine, she had a bit of a fixation on breasts. A few times she asked to see mine. Other times, she wanted to touch mine. I am a little shy and uncomfortable with showing other children my breasts. I don't know . . . call me crazy.

But I didn't want to shame or embarrass Shelly for asking, but I wanted to make sure I modeled holding firm boundaries. I gently told her that I was uncomfortable with her touching my breasts but there was nothing wrong with her curiosity.

I sat down with her parent separately and talked about an approach to address her curiosity about breasts without requiring me to show her mine. We did not want to shame her curiosity—after all, that's a natural thing for a child. So where can one find pictures of human breasts? Where is the first place a child would think to go these days? The internet: YouTube, Google, etc. But approaching this situation requires a little more preparation and planning to implement. If you sit down together to do a Google search with no advance preparation . . . well, you never know what kind of images you will find, and you might subject yourself to a really awkward situation. I googled "boobs" and "breasts" for research purposes, and it wasn't pretty; the images that appear are neither "normative" nor look like what most women have. No wonder we get such messed up impressions of what is normal.

The approach we came up with was this: we set aside a Google search to look for some classic art paintings of the female form and not just "boobs." I figured it's better to focus on the woman as a whole and not just the breasts; after all, they are just one part of a whole person. We saved some of these images in advance and then sat down together. Sitting down with your children to discuss their interest and going over it in a format they're comfortable with is meeting them where they are, right? Isn't this what children would do without a parent's direct involvement anyway? Only now you have taken some power to help guide your child in a healthy, informed, and positive manner.

I suggested a field trip to go to a museum to look at the paintings there. That way it is something they can do together and talk about the images they see, giving time to process and bring it up again in an open forum.

Children are interested in the human body, yet not many people walk around the house naked. Where are children supposed to see the things in which they are curious? And it's not just breasts children are interested in at this age.

Example 2

Around that same time, I received an email from a friend of mine who lives in the Midwest. Her daughter, Emme, was eight years old, in the second grade, loved animals, and was a smart, resourceful girl. The email from her mom went like this:

Okay, just had a talk with Emme because I borrowed her iTouch and saw that she had been on YouTube searching "an animal's penis."

As I prepared for our conversation, I totally thought of you—so I told her it was fine to be curious but that she broke our rules about using YouTube, so she has to have consequences. But since she was so honest about what she'd done and didn't blame anyone else, it was much less severe. So, my question is, what do I do about her curiosity?

I called my friend immediately and congratulated her on what I thought was a perfect response. Emme was simply curious about something and picking up on the cultural/playground cues of the word "penis" being whispered and/or being used to shock adults, she probably presumed this wasn't something to ask openly. Initially, I suggested they try sitting down together, acknowledge her curiosity, and look for penises online together, perhaps applying the classic art idea like in the example above. But I couldn't think of any images of penises in classic art paintings—the closest thing I could come up with was the statue of David by Michelangelo. Then I remembered Emme was looking for animal penises. The best series I know of that talks about the reproductive habits of animals is the one by Isabella Rossellini on Sundance.com called *Green Porno*. There are plenty of examples of various animal penises there. The *Green Porno* series is scientifically accurate and wildly entertaining. I've learned quite a bit about animal copulation myself. Ms. Rossellini is thoroughly entertaining as she singularly explains each animal and the courtship, mating, and sexual behaviors through paper costumes, puppetry, and marionette play. They are very humorous and informative, and if you can suspend your own parental embarrassment (remember your embarrassment is not your child's embarrassment), they are fascinating to watch together. I suggested my friend and her daughter check out some of these together.

Situations like these are happening every day in households all over the country. I think parents can be more attentive to their children and to what they are *not* saying out loud. You don't need to read their minds, but you should be looking for opportunities to ask them what's happening in their lives. Stay aware. Also, remember that your experiences are not their experiences. Children do not generally have the embarrassment that their parents have (although they do certainly learn that behavior quickly). Most importantly, do not punish them for their curiosity. Stop, breathe, think about what they are trying to figure out and ask them

When children are searching online or in magazines, they are curious. It's a good time to sit down together and search together. You never know what might pop up if they do a Google search on their own and you are not there to help guide things. You may need to do a little lesson planning or stacking the deck in your favor in advance, but the payoffs are rewarding.

The key phrase I have used when talking to my children about the perils of googling things is this: there are some things you can't UNSEE. Ask me and I'm happy to help you find something. It has worked so far.

Using the Internet

While I was writing the previous response to my friend, Marcia, Cindy, and I watched probably twenty of the twenty-eight *Green Porno* videos together. The girls got a little bored and wandered off after a while. About fifteen minutes later, Marcia came back into my room and asked me, "Mom, do animals have age of consent laws, too?"

Seeing that I was still sitting at my computer when she came back in, I paused for a moment and held my initial response back. I contemplated showing her the videos about bonobos from the Sex at Dawn website. I think I paused out of shame because the bonobos are pansexual; children bonobos approach adult bonobos sexually and vice versa. I do not condone pedophilia, hebephilia, etc. and I know it would be a crazy moral leap to think that somehow animal behavior gives permission or any acceptability to that behavior in humans. In that split second when I decided not to show that video, I figured it was too soon to talk about that. However, I just said in the blog, "When children ask is when to talk to them about it. I made a note to myself to cover that topic when the girls are a little older.

I stalled . . . "Um, I don't know. That's a really good question," I took a deep breath and did the best I could by saying to her, "Animals don't have laws the way people have laws. There is, I'm sure, an acceptable code of behavior and I'm sure animals know instinctively when other animals are 'ready' for courtship, mating, and sexual behavior. It may even be that they learn when they play."

I was a bit shocked at the maturity of her question—she was nine years old. I couldn't honestly recall when she and I had a conversation about age of consent laws. I think we started by talking about the age teenagers and young adults have to be to vote, drink alcohol, and have sex. She understood the voting rule. The drinking and the sex age of consent concepts seemed to puzzle her because she understands personal responsibility.

She was dumbfounded by the fact that there's an age people are "allowed" to have sex. She once said to me, "Sex is not a privilege; it cannot be taken away from us." I don't know where Marcia got it—because I never said this to her. All I could think was, "Oh, honey. I hope it stays that way." (She is aware of the efforts of some politicians and religious groups who wish to do just that—she is clear that they are doing this because they think that's what God wants).

This further reinforces the thought I have always had that children understand what you tell them. And they will remember long after you forgot you talked about it. Make sure you are honest from the beginning because, as evidenced here, it may come back to you.

Sweet Cross-Dresser

A friend of mine was a big fan of *The Rocky Horror Picture Show.* He told me he used to go to the late-night shows with his friends in high school and college, and they would all get dressed up as characters in the movie and be active participants. His costume was Dr. Frank N Furter. The mental picture of this friend dressing up in the corset, fishnet stockings, and heels always gave me a giggle; he's a tall guy with thick black hair, so I imagine he probably pulled it off very well.

Not too long ago, he and I were driving in the car together. We used to talk about my blog topics on a regular basis. This particular afternoon, I was talking about PDA and things we did as teens and *Rocky Horror* came up again. This time, I simply inquired where he got the supplies for his costume. He said, "Oh, my mom had them." I commented, "You got a corset, fishnets, and garter belts from your mom? How cool is that?!" It was as I said this that he took a huge pause . . . and realized for the first time in twenty-plus years that his mom had a corset, fishnets, and garter that he could use! He nearly drove off the road as he said, "Oh, man! My mom!" A huge wave of embarrassment seemed to wash over him as he probably got a mental image of his mom as a sexual being.

I don't want to minimize the discomfort he probably felt in thinking about his mother in this way and why she had those things, but it was so funny to witness and talk through his thought process as a sort of post-mortem. First the rationalization: there must be a function other than for sex. Then he wondered, "Why would she have these? There must be a legitimate, purposeful reason." That quickly went out the window. Then came the realization as he put two-and-two together. There are better solutions if you need stockings, so garter belts aren't necessary anymore. There isn't another decorative or symbolic use for corsets. Last came reality: it hit him like a ton of bricks, a shudder—he could now picture her wearing it and—"oh my god . . . Mom!"

I had the privilege of knowing his mom as well; she was a loving, accepting, nonjudgmental woman who raised her own children in an atmosphere where love and sex were taught without shame or guilt (the result is a grown son who respects women and is very mindful of when and with whom he is intimate). She is exactly the way I imagine lots of people wish their own mothers were. Anyway, I called her when we arrived at our destination and shared our conversation from the car ride. Her reaction was as loving and unembarrassed. We chuckled a bit at the ridiculous notion that children can't think of their parents as sexual beings. All the while, my friend was still pacing the floor as he contemplated this newfound revelation.

I enjoy this story for a couple of different reasons. First, I love that my male friend was confident enough to dress in women's lingerie. He's a hulking bear of a man, a Kinsey 0, which further disproves a number of the myths[88] about men who cross-dress. Confidence like that is sexy. Second, I am fascinated by those "ah-ha!" moments when we realize something we once thought to be true is actually not—namely, our parents were "doing it" long before we ever figured it out. Why do so many parents try to hide their love and affection for each other from their children? Shouldn't our children understand that in many cases a loving relationship is what got us here in the first place? When and why do we stop thinking of our parents as sexual beings?

Sadly, my friend doesn't dress as Dr. Frank N. Furter anymore, but it would be wonderful to see him try on this costume again!

Lasting Impression

I wanted to add something the topic of Core Erotic Theme (CET) where we develop ideas around sex and sexuality while we are young.

A friend of mine and I were discussing porn and erotic literature. We just recently uncovered that something he used to do as a tween had a profound impact on his adult sex life.

The backstory here is when he was twelve years old he began to read *Penthouse Forum* magazines. He would scan the articles and select one based on topic and length. He said articles that were too short weren't worth unzipping his fly. When he found one that was appealing, he would commence . . . do I really need to spell it out here?

This friend was particularly aroused by the stories in *Forum* that contained what we are lovingly referring to as "the change up," a typical nonsexual situation that turns into something sexual. You know, those instances where the housewife greets the pizza delivery boy and seduces him or the handy man replacing a light bulb has his pants pulled down around his ankles while he is on the ladder. It's a whole genre of "clothed female, naked male" (CFNM). Those fantasies from his youth were arousing to him then, and, until recently, he didn't realize the lasting impact this had on his sex life. Yet he packed it away into the recesses of his mind and only started unpacking because of our open discussions about turn-ons and our basic Core Erotic Themes. So now he understands why, as an adult, he still enjoys fantasizing about the neighbor's wife, being fondled while doing household chores, and for some inexplicable reason, gets aroused whenever someone delivers a pizza.

For parents of tweens: make sure you are communicating with your children about what they know or are experiencing. Do not assume your children are not exploring their own bodies. Here's some news for you . . . the National Survey of Sexual Health and

Behavior published in the *Journal of Sexual Medicine* in 2010[89] reports that by age fourteen to fifteen, 67 percent of boys had already masturbated and 13 percent of them had already received oral sex. Correspondingly, for fourteen- to fifteen-year-old girls, 43 percent had masturbated and 10 percent had received oral sex from a male. What is not clear to me from the data is if the girls had masturbated to orgasm or if they know what female orgasm is. What is wrong with girls doing this if they can derive pleasure from it?

The stuff your children are doing and seeing now is having a lasting impact on their budding sexuality. If you suppress it, repress it, or otherwise make sex shameful, it may have an adverse effect on how they express themselves sexually as adults. If you talk about fantasy etc. now, they are more likely to have a healthier, sex-positive attitude when they are adults.

Of course, this is tough stuff! As a mother, I get nervous thinking of my own daughters engaging in sexual behavior at what seems to be a young age. I want to make sure I keep their little life rafts moored to the mother ship so they always know they can come to me with questions and that I'll do my best to answer them. It's okay to acknowledge your discomfort. It's okay to say you don't know the answer but offer to research it together. But please do not lie or make things up. It only pushes your children away from you. If you lie to them and they find out the "real" answer, you will have proven to them that you don't know what you are talking about. Our children already think they know it all, let them at least know the truth.

I want you to remember your own youth. Remember how awkward and uncomfortable it was dealing with all of those hormones and breast buds and first periods or cracking voices and facial hair and growing pains. Did you go through all that alone? Wouldn't it have been better if a loving, caring adult in your life talked to you about it? Okay, of course, lots of you are going to cringe at the thought of your own uncool parent discussing sex, but are you so uncool yourself? I know plenty of adults who would rather have someone else have these conversations with their children for them. Don't you want to stay informed and involved?

Also think, when are your kids more likely to engage in risky behavior—when they are informed and can make decisions without shame, or otherwise?

Combining the Blocks

The surest way to corrupt a youth is to instruct them to hold in higher esteem those who think alike than those who think differently.

~ Friedrich Nietzsche

As you can tell from the book to this point, the blocks I have identified do not always stand alone. Many times, they work together and help to illustrate ways we can approach the difficult topic of human sexuality with our families with much less fear. And that's one of my biggest points: I want us to move away from using fear as a tactic to teach about sex. What do I mean? Think about how we teach children about sex versus how we teach about something like the kitchen stove. Typically, a parent starts with a warning: they tell babies and toddlers, "Don't touch. Hot!" We do not explain in detail to them the specific consequences. But as the child gets older and we are more comfortable with the child's grasp of the danger behind the words "hot" and the power of this appliance, we give more specific instructions as to how, when, and why they should be careful. We specify when the stove is on, when a burner is lit, or an indicator light is illuminated that means the stove is hot. It varies by parent, but as children become tweens or teens many parents begin to teach them that the stove can be used in ways that are beneficial. Children need to understand the stove's power and potential before they can use it. Teaching a little bit at a time in a gradual approach is a great way to ease into the more complex stuff later. As you can see, how we teach our children about the stove using reason, logic, and empathy is a great strategy.

The same goes for learning about sex and sexual behaviors. What don't we do when we teach our children about the stove? Do people show toddlers pictures of third-degree burns to make a point about what could happen if the child touched the stove? I would not show my children those types of photos to control their behavior. We wouldn't think to use the worst-case scenario to scare children from touching or using the stove. I don't understand the reasoning behind using a worst-case scenario approach to teach children about sex either. Yet the sex-negative equivalent of that is used in many sex education classes. You know the one—you may have even experienced it in your sex ed classes when you were growing up—the lesson when students are shown pictures of the various Sexually Transmitted Infections (STIs)—various stages of syphilis, gonorrhea, herpes, genital warts. Trying to scare them doesn't have the intended effect. It may gross a person out at first, but inevitably, one gets past it and goes back to thinking, "Oh, that won't happen to me." Let's go back to figuring out a reasonable and logical way to teach c about human sexual behavior while keeping empathy in the equation.

And remember that trying to scare someone out of doing something doesn't work. A meta-analysis, published in 2002, of Scared Straight[90] programs found that type of intervention to be more harmful than doing nothing, and actually *increases* the likelihood of delinquency than youths who were not exposed to that program. By extension, it shows me that fear, scaring, or punishment are not good methods of behavior modification when it comes to teaching about sex.

Talking about sex in the context of relationships and mutual pleasure as it relates to sex is important. Remember, sexuality is natural. It's a normal human behavior like eating. There is no need to try to scare people from having sex when you give them information that is useful in a measured, little-by-little approach.

In this chapter, I will begin with a deeply personal blog I wrote in two parts. The second part includes what I think we can do together to see real change to some of the issues that exist around human sexuality today. I give you fair warning that this is a pretty solemn and serious portion in comparison to the entire book so far.

Educating About Sex in a "Rape Culture"

Full disclosure: the words you are about to read are from a person who identifies as a feminist, is a board-certified sexologist and sex educator who through education and communication wants all people to have happy, healthy, pleasurable sex lives, who is a mother of children, and who was once raped.

It's been a while since I've written a blog as The MamaSutra; this one in particular has taken me nearly one year to feel ready to hit "send." The issues herein (sexual assault, "rape culture" and media influences on same, consent and boundaries, etc.) continue to garner spotlights in our news and politics. One recent occurrence came in January 2014 when the White House issued a renewed call to action[91] and the "1 is 2 Many" Public Service Announcement[92] about sexual assault on campus. Doing so seems to have made this issue a political hot topic. I know this is a sensitive issue that riles up a lot of emotion and opinion. Everyone is absolutely entitled to his or her opinions about this topic, but I have colleagues who have experienced extreme hostility after writing about this toward both themselves and their families. Knowing this has made me question whether to publish this anonymously or not; this is why it took me a year to publish.

This is a two-part post. In this first part, I will tell you situations I believe contribute to American society being a Culture of Humiliation and Disrespect (I prefer this phrase over what others call a "rape culture"). For the purposes of this blog, my definition is as follows:

1. A culture that mutely and blindly refuses to acknowledge behavior that supports victim blaming and protects abusers and rapists

2. Forgets to look at the causes that lead to the acceptance of violence against others, including rape, in our society

3. Sexualizes or punishes other beings for being just that—something "other"

4. Refuses to see the humanity of others by reducing them to mere objects or body parts

To describe how I think we got to where we are today, let's start with some basic ingredients:

- Start with a society obsessed with all things SEX.

- Take away honest, accurate sexual education.

- Deny real talk about consent and deny discovering or expressing your boundaries out of misguided politeness.
- Make sure that REAL information about sex and sexuality is difficult to find.
- Place a stigma or shame on anyone who is interested in healthy sex.
- Add the death of discourse—an inability to talk about sex, sexuality, etc.
- Broadcast the idea that sex is just for procreation and/or just about penises and vaginas.
- Only acknowledge one narrow, hetero-centric view of what sex is and how sex should be.
- Forget about the fact that there are critical, nonsexual components to sex that are important for everyone to learn.
- Fill the media with all manner of sex-negative or inaccurate sex information.
- *Stir.*

So, where do people see this humiliation and disrespect in action?

Let's review a couple of examples looking through the eyes of a young person who has never had sex ed or has never learned some basic concepts about boundaries or consent. (Because let's face it, even if you have had basic sex ed, were you also taught about communication? consent? respect? pleasure? fantasy?)

Situation 1

This person watches season two, episode one, "Don't Trust The B—In Apt 23." Six minutes into this episode, the main female character muses about how fun it is to shoot a hot guy with a tranquilizer gun and hear his body hit the ground, then this character says dreamily, "Tranq Sex: it's consensual."

I'm sorry, but no! No one points out what was just said was wrong or why. Does anyone point out that tranquilizer sex is the opposite of consensual and that it constitutes rape? No. It gets the laughs and they move on. Perhaps it was supposed to be funny or acceptable because it was a woman saying it and not a man? Well, it wasn't funny to me. I was horrified. Think of the kids who saw that and the implied message they received absent of any redirect.

Situation 2

This person watches the movie *Bachelorette* (2012). In this movie, Joe, who has been long interested in Katie. Forty-three minutes into the movie, they are all out late partying at a strip club. As they are leaving, the player-type guy friend tells Joe that Katie (who is puking and falling down drunk) is "G2G—Good to Go, so just take her home and slip it in." Joe replies, "I am not going to 'slip it in.' She is wasted, that would be like rape." (side note: WTF?! " . . . would be like rape?" THAT IS RAPE!). This guy friend gives Joe a bottle of pills, and Joe whispers to ask if the pills are date rape drugs. The player guy tells him loudly no, it's Xanax for him to take so he won't be so paranoid.

This scene is clearly giving a really disturbing message! No one in the movie addresses why any of that is messed up. The message is that the man is supposed to numb himself so he doesn't have to feel bad for raping a woman who can't give consent herself because she is clearly intoxicated. Can anyone describe that to me differently?

(Side note: I don't even look for these examples anymore. It's like they find me. Either that or this stuff is so prevalent that no matter what I watch I see it. This scares me because I don't watch TV much. Really. Someone else will have to tell me if I'm off base--that this is only a chance happening that I'm stumbling onto these examples as often as I do . . . but I really doubt it.)

These examples are cumulative.

Let me say this very clearly: I believe it is absolutely irresponsible for our society to provide the "entertainment" content we do under the guise of "humor" when our youth is not also exposed to accurate, honest education around sex and sexuality. How does anyone understand that something is or is not funny if they don't also understand the message behind it? This education is not just for children. I know plenty of adults who have difficulty with not only their emotions, feelings, and thoughts about sexual behavior but also need to understand the nonsexual components behind sex, love, and relationships. Our understanding of this cannot improve if there is no solid foundation.

Why do I think some guys rape?

The men I am going to describe here—and I'm only going to address the men here, although women do rape as well—are the ones where the words "nice guy" have been used (see also the teens in the Steubenville rape trial). I am not addressing the clearly sociopathic ones, but I will touch on that later.

There is a blog that came out not long ago which says there are two kinds of rapists: "sadistic and opportunistic." I believe there are more than just two kinds of rapists as that blog would have us think. This binary thinking around rape is bogus (just like any binary thinking about gender, sexual orientation, the range of sexual behaviors, etc. is bogus). I believe it's a spectrum, like most things. And none of the rape spectrum is good. I know there are sociopaths who are on their way to more violent behavior (like murder). There are other men who just don't care what women think and want to take what they think is theirs to take but who aren't necessarily on their way to murder (a result of our objectification of women and/or the goal-focused approach to sex—a.k.a. "get in, get off, get out"). But there are also men who truly don't know or who aren't aware of their behavior to know that what they are doing is wrong (Steubenville?).

The TV and movie situations listed above are part of a much bigger machine that fails to inform. I think we can use these and other examples to help us identify why rape may be happening right in front of us. It seems because what happened in Steubenville was not the "violent" form of nonconsensual sex it was not seen as rape. Does this happen just because we have failed as a society to inform our population accurately about the importance of good sexual information? Whose fault is this? Is fault even the right concept? Some people wish others would stop blaming and getting angry, but that is part of the healing process. It's hard, and lots of people don't know how to move through that with grace and responsibility. But no matter where you are in your journey, the thing that needs to be addressed is "How do we fix this?"

How do we transform this Culture of Humiliation and Disrespect?

I mentioned earlier that I am a victim of rape myself. I am not comfortable describing that situation here. I will, however, tell you about another story that happened to me not long ago.

This next part might be uncomfortable to read as it deals with issues of consent. One night, a guy I was in a relationship with had a few drinks (he was drunk, but he and I disagreed on what "drunk" was). Normally I'm up for sex, but we had been arguing about something and things surrounding that issue had not yet been resolved. When we went to bed, he wanted to have sex (I did not). I was laying on my side, turned away from him. He proceeded to pressure me: pressing up against me, rolling me over onto my back, and clearly presenting--ahem ahem—that he wanted to have sex. Besides my body language, I told him verbally that I wasn't interested in having sex and told him to go to sleep, yet he persisted. It got to a point where I got so angry that I sat up and said, "Knock it off!

If you don't stop right now, you will be raping me!" He stopped immediately, appeared a bit disoriented, mumbled (apologies?), and passed out.

I was very upset and called a girlfriend the next day to tell her what happened. Also, I had a follow-up conversation with him, and he did not remember the situation at all.

At one point in my time with him, I cared for him very deeply. He seemed to be a good man and was a father himself. I will say it again: to all outward appearances, this person seemed like a good man. But if I may suggest, he seemed a little unaware and numb. I do not believe this person is terrible nor unredeemable. But this example fits the behavior of a person who had absolutely no sex education in his entire school career (which he did not). So, where did he learn about sexual behaviors, pleasure-focused intimacy, consent, and boundaries? Where does anyone who doesn't get the education from a good sex-positive source learn it?

Next, I will detail my suggestions for what we must do to eliminate rape culture. Ours is a culture steeped in a deep disrespect for women, not to mention a disrespect for any "other," and for some reason, for many there exists an absolute inability to listen when something has a "feminist" undertone. Many people fight the notion that "rape culture" exists. Perhaps the idea, and the real pain behind it, is too difficult to grasp, so it is easier to deny.

Situations come up from time to time, like Steubenville, rapes on university campuses, etc., that scare me to no end. I find myself unable to even read the accounts without getting extremely upset, if only for the depictions of utter disrespect and stupidity on all levels. I know these are not isolated events. I know there are plenty of kids out there who think rape is only rape when it's violent or think it's only rape when drugs are present or it's at a party. Just because many people think that rape is only rape when it's the drag-you-into-the-bushes-and-kill-you kind does not make it so. Let's take action where we need to and punish those who rape. But let's also try to figure out how to educate everyone and to fix this so it doesn't continue to happen!

I believe the best sex education starts in a very basic manner and really has nothing to do with genitals. To help people understand the nonsexual components of human sexuality, I have identified my Five Building Blocks to a Healthy Sexuality (Communication, Consent, Respect, Pleasure, and Fantasy). My model has not been part of a research study with an independent review board, yet I look forward to peer review and any feedback on these. I have identified these blocks based on the observations of a sexologist, sex educator, and mother. If you break down the problems we have in our society right now with sex and sexuality—not only rape culture—these problems could be addressed by thinking about the Five Building Blocks as a foundation for where we start to educate people about sex and sexuality. Again, the important thing to note is that none of these blocks have anything directly to do with genitals, but they absolutely are part of where we start to teach young people. It doesn't matter if you are a person who believes in comprehensive sex education or abstinence-only before marriage sex education, these blocks apply to both approaches. They are also absolutely for everyone at any age, and you can start learning them at any time. Now would be good.

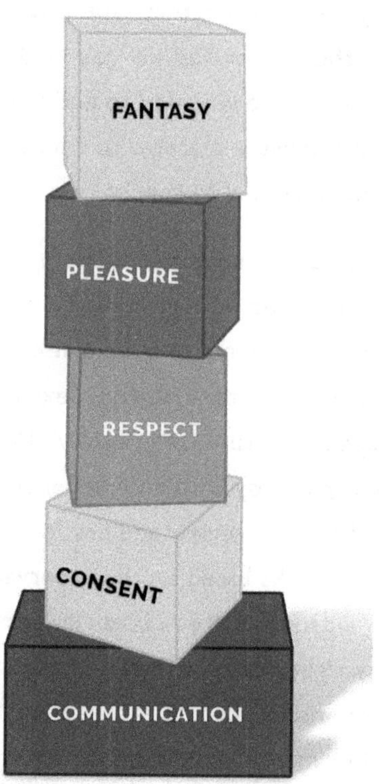

The Five Building Blocks to a Healthy Sexuality

Here's a summary of what I've said (if you want more information, look at the corresponding chapter). It is not enough to say that "people should just know these things" or that it's part of being a good human being. I think rape exists because no one has taught anyone about the importance of these five blocks:

1. **Communication**: Being able to communicate feelings and emotions, understanding that emotion is not a bad thing, communicating needs, wants, desires and listening to the

same in others, tuning in to the body language of others, communication through touch, encouraging and modeling communication (in general), and using correct terminology.

2. **Consent**: The importance of boundaries; learning ownership of your own body; embracing and exercising the ability to say "no," and being able to accept "no" for an answer.

3. **Respect**: Having a healthy respect for self and for others; learning a healthy body image and being okay with nakedness; extending the concept of "do no harm" (along with consent); a shift in talking about "virginity."

4. **Pleasure**: The simple power of human touch like a hug; knowing that pleasure is more than just "sexual;" recognition that any sexual pleasure should be there for all parties, not just one person (which is usually the male).

5. **Fantasy**: It's important you encourage and maintain a child-like curiosity and focus, understanding that what we learn about sex, outside of formal education, is fantasy; it's okay to have fantasies and they don't all have to be acted upon or fulfilled.

When we can teach these things to our children, they learn skills that they can apply to their relationships as they grow and develop. How many of us could have used these lessons growing up?

Here's another piece of my own suggested solution:

- Let's remember that sex is not just about penises and vaginas.

- Let's teach people that communicating their feelings early and often is better than creating situations in which people take frustration out on others because there is no other outlet.

- Let's remove the stigma around asking for help or advice. There is absolutely nothing wrong with asking for help or getting help. If you ask any sex therapist, educator, or counselor, most people just want to know that they are "normal" sexually.

- Let's call out when shows and movies depict things like what happened in the two situations that I outlined in Part I, maybe taking a page from the Miss Representation organization's #NotBuyingIt campaign.

- Let's make sure people know it is absolutely okay to share your feelings. Allowing a young boy to cry does not "turn him gay." It tells him that it's okay to have emotion. Allowing any child to cry is okay, especially when there is a hug there to hold them while they cry.

- Let's allow our children to see us cry. It does not show them we are weak; it shows them that we are human. We can help by showing them what they can do to feel better—stuffing those emotions down is not it.

- Let's make sure people know it is absolutely okay to share their heart openly and that they are whole beings in and of themselves who do not need another half, better or otherwise. If someone doesn't take their heart, it is the other person's loss, not their own.

- Let's make sure everyone understands pleasure-focused intimacy and that when you engage in sexual behavior, pleasure is to be had by all parties involved (and that pleasure might look different to us all and we must be able to communicate that as well). It certainly is not about one party "getting off." Learning that ejaculation is the result before pregnancy occurs (if our kids get that much info), it's no wonder so many people have unfulfilled sex lives. How much fun is it if only one partner ever gets off? Answer: none!

- Let's teach people how to read their own emotional responses—clean up your messes, leave no trace.

These suggestions are just the tip of the iceberg and are really focused only lightly on the first two blocks: Communication and Consent. Each of the five is vitally important to the conversations and lessons about sex and sexuality.

Many parents have a difficult time approaching the topic of sex with their children. It's understandable: not many of us got good sex education as we were growing up. I think parents need to realize that the conversations that lead up to the tougher questions about sex and sexuality are so basic, the concepts that need to be discussed are so elementary. These Five Building Blocks to a Healthy Sexuality are it. Our children learn math and some of its basic concepts when they are toddlers. You don't start with calculus. You start first with things like one block, two blocks, etc. Then over time, we teach them how to add and subtract. Hopefully, they've gotten those concepts down when we add into the mix multiplication and division—and so on. The same approach follows with discussions about sex and sexuality. You start with more basic concepts. That is what I propose here.

In our American society, if we talk about sex at all we certainly don't talk about the pleasure of sex—making it clear to everyone that sex should be enjoyable for all parties involved. Instead, we make it scary. We don't talk about the benefits of sex—that orgasms can improve immune function. Instead, we talk about the dangers.

I want to shift this. Thankfully, I know I'm not alone in this wish. I want to make sure that we educate our children and adults about ALL aspects of human sexual behavior—the who, the what, the why, and the how—so everyone can develop and enjoy healthy sexuality.

Practical Tips

A lesson taught with humor is a lesson retained.

~ Dr. Ruth Westheimer, quoting the Talmud

How is it possible to talk to our children about sexuality in a way that doesn't evoke such anxiety in ourselves? This topic brings up so much emotion for people, which shows up in so many different behaviors. I think there are five things to keep in mind as one begins these conversations:

1. Breathe

Relax and know that your anxiety or nervousness about this topic is not your child's. Relaxing may not do much to ease your own discomfort at the moment. Do your best to stay present and don't allow yourself to be paralyzed. Sex is a topic that has so much to do with helping your child develop into healthy adult sexuality.

Adults sexualize nonsexual situations. A child touching their genitals is not the same goal-oriented experience we adults may have come to identify as masturbation, but again, our own experience is not our child's experience. Sometimes children are just simply exploring—do you have parts that are different than what I have? Stumbling upon toddlers playing doctor with each other, a calm response or redirection works positively for the children's natural curiosity (which you can then talk to the child about what they wanted to know or see) as opposed to a parent's shocked reaction (which can emotionally scar a child).

Be aware. Other times parents overlook things too that adults would consider sexual in same-sex situations as well. Sleepovers are places children talk, share, and learn as well. It's not just the opposite-sex sleepovers where experimentation happens—and even then, sometimes nothing happens. I'm not telling you this to scare you or make you want to put your child in a bubble. I want to make you aware that talking to your child is important, as is trusting your child.

Realize you are not alone. There are a lot of parents out there who want to do the right thing. Others just don't know what to say/do or when. That's where having good resources comes in. There are lots of sex-positive sex educators out there who have answers to your questions. There are also educators that I would consider sex-negative, and the information they share does more harm than good in my opinion. Sometimes it's as simple as knowing whom to ask. There is a fantastic group of sexologist colleagues and friends that I lovingly call The League of Sex-Positive Heroes who also write within this sex educating space that I think very highly of their work (see Appendix A). There is an educator for every audience and subject.

2. Plan Ahead

Parents, talk to each other. Do either of you have a history of what worked (or didn't work) for you when you were growing up? Make a plan to figure out who will say what. According to sexual health educator Amy Lang,[93] boys want to hear about sex from dad and about relationships from mom. Girls want to hear about the physical changes, etc. from mom and about relationships from dad. But if you do not have both genders in your household, don't worry about refraining from covering those topics; your children still want to hear from you because you are their parents.

There is never a perfect time to talk about sex. Waiting for the right time to talk to your child about sex is sort of like waiting for the right time to have a baby—most people like to think that they can plan when to get pregnant but are often unable to do so. Sometimes, when puberty education starts in school (most often fourth or fifth grade!), parents want to coordinate having "The Talk" with their children. Waiting until a child is nine or ten years old is waiting too long—but if you have waited, please start now. Pro tip: when a child is strapped into a seat belt, they becomes a captive audience. There are plenty of opportunities to chat if you become adept at identifying them.

Try to give only accurate, honest information to your child. This applies to you as a parent supplying incorrect information as well. You may think you are protecting your child but in reality, it is not. Giving them incorrect information will only undermine you as an authority. Be honest. Make it simple, one sentence as best you can. Let the child drive the next question.

Respect your child's emotional intelligence. Most parents refuse to think about their children as one day being grown up and sexual.

As much as we would love for them to remain children forever, they will grow up, hopefully with your guidance and communication. Don't get too ahead of yourself though. The reality is this is going to happen whether you want that or not. They're still children but yes, some day I imagine you will want them to enjoy healthy adult sexuality. Maybe even better than you have it?

When it comes to sex, most adults want to know that they're "normal." Children are no different. This is why they ask questions about your own experiences. They often want to know how old you were when you got your period, when did your boobs start growing, and the age at which a boy starts to have wet dreams. They just want a point of comparison to make sure everything is happening when they think it's supposed to happen. Puberty in particular can have such a huge range for the age at first onset. Early bloomers get anxiety about being first, thinking there's something wrong with them. Late bloomers worry there's something wrong with them because things aren't changing yet. Tell them your story, and they most likely will relax a bit. Chances are they will follow you or their other parent in terms of development but then again, maybe they won't. They are all individuals.

3. Start Talking Early and Do So Often

This is not just for your child's benefit—it's for your benefit too. Attaining a sense of ease and comfort around the basic words is a wonderful thing when the more difficult conversations will come. Starting in infancy when you are changing diapers, a parent can say, "I'm wiping the urine off your penis" or "Let's get that anus clean" or "Looks like you need some diaper rash cream on your vulva." Get used to saying the proper names now. It's okay to acknowledge how awkward it is. Trust me that it gets easier later.

Reframe if it's easier. Think about these conversations this way: our children learn math and some of its basic concepts when they are toddlers. First with things like one block, two blocks, etc. Then over time we teach them how to add and subtract. Hopefully, they've gotten those concepts down when we add into the mix multiplication and division—and so on. The same approach follows with discussions about sex and sexuality. You can't teach a child basic math when they already know multiplication. You can't wait until they're fifteen to squeeze in a five-year course in math. Depriving them of the basics early on makes them giggly and shy later. They're not asking certain questions when they're shy and embarrassed.

Talk to your faith leaders and schools. Make sure the information they are giving to children about sex and sexuality is accurate and honest, and if they take a position on something, make sure they own the motivations behind their teachings. Make sure neither church nor school is lying to the children. The cost of finding out the "authorities" were incorrect can undermine that authority and the respect for same. In other words, chances are your children won't go back to that resource again. **This applies for you as a parent supplying incorrect information as well.

Praise your child for coming to you. "I'm glad you asked" or "Goodness, I'm going to need a second to think about that" is a great way to stall and take a moment to get your thoughts together before moving on to the question at hand. You can even ask, "What do you think the answer is?" but not in a sarcastic tone that kids can pick up on. This also can buy you some time to respond. But then, give an answer to your child. The shock of the initial question may have you wanting to ask, "Where'd you hear that?" or "Who told you that?" You're totally allowed to ask those questions, but please don't make that your first response. It comes across as accusatory and may have the child rethinking their choice to go to you. Of course, you can ask about their source after you give your answer to your child. But if you do, consider why you want to know and what you will do with the information you receive back.

One strategy is **answering questions as they come up.** Alternately, you can bring up the topic when you see something noteworthy, like an ad on TV or a billboard along the road. Even better, when it isn't a good example, talk about what makes it a poor example. I have written many times about these types of scenarios with my children—and it's not always about genitalia or intercourse. Lots of times it's about sexism, double standards, status quo, how things are different now than when I was a kid. My children are sometimes fascinated by those stories, and it pleases me to hear their responses as well.

If you're wondering what they know, then ask. To find out what your child knows about sex, the simplest way to find out is to ask them. "You know, I was curious about this thing no one wanted to talk about when I was a kid. And I know you have more access to info online than I ever did. What do you know so far or what do you have questions about?" You might even pose this question right along with any of the books by Robie Harris. They are great books to read along with your child or to leave with your child to examine at their own pace.

4. Know Why You Feel the Way You Do About Sex

Please take the initiative to **examine for yourself why you feel the way you do** about sex and sexuality—especially if you are preaching something other than what you practiced in your own personal life. I have heard too many second- and third-hand stories of men who slept with many women without using birth control, only to get one pregnant, ask her to have an abortion, and then later "find God" to help them repent their sins. As a result, they go a bit the other way in their expectations of what their own children should and shouldn't do sexually. We commonly know this as "do as I say, not as I do."

Be strong. Keep in mind that avoiding these important conversations makes children vulnerable. Pedophiles shape children to be silent and secretive. So, if parents are framing sex to be secretive or shameful, then parents can unwittingly lay a foundation for their children to be unable to talk about it if or when things happen sexually without shame or guilt. Think about our culture of humiliation and disrespect; lots of women don't come forward because they fear they won't be believed or that somehow they asked for it. Our children don't deserve to feel like this if they need help.

Remember frame of reference. That first touch of their genitals as infants may have been a random act, but the fact that touching those parts feels good is not random. It's pleasurable. Children touch their genitals because it feels good. Once it feels good, classical conditioning and learning begin. It will cause them to want to feel good again. Our genitals are always with us, within arm's reach, and—hey, how about that—those opposable thumbs really come in handy! The shame begins that first time a parent yells, slaps their hand away, or otherwise stops the behavior in an abrupt, shaming way. It's easy enough to whisper, "Honey, that's something people do in the privacy of their bedroom or bathroom at home," if the child is touching themselves in a public place. The best you can do is give your child information about place and hygiene. Yes, it feels good and it's okay for them to touch their own body, but it's best to do that with clean hands and in a place where they are not going to be disturbed or where they might disturb others. Consider this: If you were caught doing something you didn't realize you shouldn't be doing, wouldn't you want someone to redirect you in the most polite, quiet way possible?

Physical touch feels good. **Not all touch is sexual touch.** I do not believe Freud was correct in his theory about the latency stage of sexuality. I have noticed more interest, inquiries, and understanding from my tween-aged daughter than I ever would have expected. My child is not alone either. There are lots of parents in my daughter's grade who expressed the same realization. Of course, it's not universal; there are plenty of children of the same age who haven't shown any sort of outward interest, at least none that the parents have picked up on. As a society, we do plenty to shame each other. Do we really want to do this to our children too? Sex has the potential of being a truly wonderful experience. However, since most of us didn't have that experience, we can't conceive of it for others either.

Breathe again. Heaven forbid a father has to think that one day his daughter may wish to enjoy sexual activities, or a mother think that her son is going to leave her for someone else. Okay, plenty of years for that, we're talking about the here and now. They're still children, but if I had to venture a guess, you want your child to have good, happy, positive experiences to develop healthy adult sexuality. Experiences as good as you had—perhaps even better than you had.

If all else fails, get help. Children respect when you need to call in reinforcements, and it teaches them that it's okay to ask for help if they need it as well. Parents can't be expected to know every answer to the questions our children have all the time. There are people who know more about lots of things than you do. It doesn't mean you are a failure or anything like that. It simply acknowledges that everyone has their strengths, and we can use the resources available to us to get the answers we need.

5. Keep It Simple

Lots of parents think that talking to children about sex is about sexual positions, defining terms right off the bat, etc. To me, it's more basic than that. There are Five Building Blocks to a Healthy Childhood Sexuality: communication, consent, respect, pleasure, and fantasy. These are the core concepts that a parent should keep in mind when talking to their children about sex. It's more all-encompassing than just sexual positions and sex terms and other technical sex stuff. One of the wonderful effects of learning about these blocks is this: in many instances, the examples I give are ones where the lessons learned can apply to one or more of the blocks. A lesson that appears on the surface to be about consent can also provide learning about respect. Or pleasure.

Please note that the underlying theme in all of the reasons listed in chapter 1 is shame. It is self-driven. Researcher Brené Brown did a TED Talk on shame[94] in March of 2012. In her talk, Ms. Brown said, "The thing to understand about shame is it's not guilt. Shame is a focus on self, guilt is a focus on behavior. Shame is "I am bad." Guilt is "I did something bad." She explains:

> *"Shame is an epidemic in our culture. And to get out from underneath it, to find our way back to each other, we have to understand how it affects us and how it affects the way we're parenting [. . .] If we're going to find our way back to each other, we have to understand and know empathy, because empathy's the antidote to shame. If you put shame in a petri dish, it needs three things to grow exponentially: secrecy, silence, and judgment. If you put the same amount of shame in a petri dish and douse it with empathy, it can't survive. The two most powerful words when we're in struggle: me too."*
> *~ Brené Brown, Listening to Shame, TED Talk, March 2012*

I would say there are dozens of more good reasons why parents should talk to their children than find excuses not to. There is plenty of incorrect information out there, and would it be so bad if a child has the right information? In my opinion, as long as you are sharing accurate information, how does a child lose?

Conclusion

When I tell people I am a sex educator, I have had people say to me with a bit of a swagger, "Oh, I already know all there is to know about that topic." When that happens, I want to ask them if their partner would agree with them.

I see this ignorant bravado alongside innocent lack of understanding about what sex and sexuality really are time and again. I thought I knew a lot about sex until I began to study the topic academically; turns out, I really didn't know anything. And I'm guessing the people who respond in such a cocky manner don't either.

We all have stories about our own sex education (or lack thereof). It does not matter whom I tell what I'm doing with my life; everyone has a story that is important about sexuality and about what they've experienced in their life up to this point that they want to share. I talked with my accountant about their grandkids' sexuality, with an online tech support person in India about societal differences in dealing with sexuality, and with a banker about how early to start the conversations with children. One woman, who was a bit older than me, was told by her own mother that pregnancy was caused by kissing. She said she was so afraid to kiss her own father and brothers after that!

Misinformation does not protect a child, but it can give them anxiety about something else. Our histories are important, and we can figure out ways to share our experiences. However, our experiences are not the experiences of our children; they will have their own stories, but ideally, they will get better information than we did.

Sex education as it is in many places around the country focuses on just three areas: select areas of anatomy and physiology, reproductive biology, and pregnancy/STI prevention. Your children (and you for your relationships) deserve to have so much more information than just this.

I hope this book helps you to raise children into aware and sexually aware young adults who make good decisions about their sexuality (knowing all of this is more broadly defined than just the act of having sex).

There are many more good reasons why parents SHOULD talk to their children as opposed to finding excuses not to. There is plenty of incorrect information out there, and we have generations of people who have stumbled through life without accurate sex education. It is time we begin to do what's right. They say, "If it ain't broke, don't fix it." I believe this has been broken for so long. Would it be so bad if a child has the right info for a change? Can we try a new approach since the old one has not worked? In my opinion, as long as you are sharing accurate information, how does a child lose?

Talk with your children about what they want to do—be careful not to make the mistake of telling your kid about what you want them to do. When they give ideas and you don't like them, it's okay to ask, "Okay, what else?" but do not expect them to always make the choice you would. To some extent, parenting is giving children all the information you can so they will feel empowered and knowledgeable enough to go out and make good decisions on their own. We will not be able to be with our children all the time. Build muscle memory in this area a little at a time. Practice with smaller decisions and that will give both you and your child confidence with the bigger stuff. And hopefully, this book has given you an understanding of the benefits and inspiration for the behavioral skills needed for using a gradual information method of teaching about sexuality.

My experience with learning about sex and sexuality was like many of your experiences. When I was a young person growing up, my friends and I didn't get quality information about sex and sexuality from the people who mattered to us. I wanted to change that; if I can help people achieve a healthy, happy sex life, and they can pass their knowledge along to their children and their children's children . . . well, that would please me to no end.

I am not a person to invoke God to try to convince others to listen to me; I do believe I have been put on this earth to do this work. Everything I have learned, seen, or experienced has brought me to this point. I see my role as being here to help and give you the tools and tips you need:

1. For your own sex life.
2. To give you the confidence to be able to talk to the young people in your life.

I want to thank you for reading this book, and I hope you have more comfort in being able to break all of these issues up into bite-sized pieces. It's so much easier when you don't feel pressure to tackle the topic of sex all in one sitting.

Your fear about this topic is real and valid. I'm here to help you understand that talking about sex and sexuality is not as bad as it seems. Using the five building blocks described in this book, you can help the young people in your life by giving them information that will help them make good decisions as they grow and develop healthy adult sexuality.

Thank you!

xxoo

Lanae

The MamaSutra

Enjoy This book?

Head over to **www.themamasutra.net/readmebonus** to find bonus material for this book.

I realize when I am excited and motivated after reading a book, I love to search the web and find more resources on the subject. I've prepared such a place for you to begin. By following this link, you'll get exclusive access to content that accompanies this book. There are lists of resources and links mentioned in the book as well as courses, conversation starters, and other fun downloads, and more on my site. You can even dive deeper into my blog posts by searching for any of the five building blocks for more examples of how to put these concepts to work for you.

I'll be adding more courses and material to my site over time. To help guide you through, check back often so you can get the latest ideas for making these conversations fun and easy.

Appendix A

Sex-Positive Parents Additional Resources

"League of Sex-Positive Heroes"

1. More **Sex-Positive Parenting Experts:**
   Logan Levkoff, loganlevkoff.com
   Airial Clark, thesexpositiveparent.com
   Al Vernacchio, alvernacchio.com
   Remi Newman, healthysexforlife.com
   Nadine Thornhill, nadinethornhill.com
   Amy Lang, birdsandbeesandkids.com
   Anya Manes, talkingaboutsex.com
   Kenna Cook, panpolyprincess.com
   Christopher Pepper, mrhealthteacher.com
   Julia Feldman, givingthetalk.com
   Dolly Klock, adolessonsLA.com
   Melissa Pinter Carnagey, sexpositivefamilies.com
   Raising Kids Without Sexual Shame,
   facebook.com/KidsNoShame/

2. **Sex-Positive Podcasts** (where you can find parenting covered too)
   Sex Talk with My Mom
   TheSexEd.com
   Six Minute Sex Ed by Kim Cavill

3. **Sex-Positive Parenting Books:**
   Robie Harris series
   Judith Levine, *Harmful to Minors*
   Rosalind Wiseman, *Queen Bees and Wannabes*
   Peggy Orenstein, *Cinderella Kidnapped My Daughter* and *Girls and Sex*
   Cory Silverberg, *What Makes a Baby* and *Sex Is a Funny Word*
   Al Vernacchio, *For Goodness Sex*
   Logan Levkoff, *Third Base Ain't What It Used to Be* and *Got Teens?*
   Rowan Murphy, *For Foxes Sake*
   Heather Corinna, *SEX: All You Need to Know Sexuality Guide*
   Laura Berman, *Talking to Your Kids About Sex*
   Dr. Ruth Westheimer, *Dr. Ruth's Guide to Teens and Sex Today*

4. **Sex-Positive Organizations and Websites:**
   The Center for Sex Education (sexedcenter.org)
   PlannedParenthood.org
   Sexuality Information and Education Council of the United States (SIECUS.org)
   ThePornConversation.com
   UnHushed.org

5. **Great Organizations for Developing Adolescents:**
   Scarleteen.com
   TheTrevorProject.org
   Amaze.org
   AdvocatesForYouth.com
   Girls Leadership (girlsleadershipinstitute.org)
   About-Face (about-face.org)
   NoH8 Campaign (noh8campaign.com)
   The Representation Project (therepresentationproject.org)
   TheBareTalk.com
   Genderspectrum.org

6. **Organizations to Get Help for Violence or Abuse:**
   RAINN (Rape, Abuse, and Incest National Network)
   National Sexual Violence Resource Center (NSVRC)

Appendix B

Brief Glossary

Children = All beings under the age of eighteen, including infants. toddlers, tweens, and teens.

Enlightenment = Sex education that results in understanding and the spread of knowledge.

Gender = Many different things: gender identity, gender expression, biological sex at birth, sexual orientation.

Kinsey Scale = A scale (published in 1948) of a person's self-declared sexual orientation on a seven-point continuum. A person with exclusively heterosexual experiences is a ten or exclusively homosexual experiences is a six. This is inadequate today because there is no rating for those who identify as asexual.

Parents = Adults and caregivers in a child's life. Not limited to blood relation, but all who have a vested interest in the healthy development of children as autonomous and independent beings.

Promiscuous = A judgmental term meaning someone having more sex than you are.

Sex = What we do. The behaviors.

Sex Positive = An attitude towards human sexuality that regards all consensual sexual activities as fundamentally healthy and pleasurable and encourages sexual pleasure and experimentation. Or very simply, being comfortable with one's own sexuality and with sexuality in general.

Sexual Debut = What is traditionally called "virginity." This term allows for a broader and self-defined determination of the beginning of one's sexual life and allows for more points to celebrate different rites of passage (again, self-defined).

Sexuality = Part of our life from birth until death.

"Unwanted Sexual Contact" = What is traditionally called "sexual abuse." Changing the term to this makes the child or person in this situation feel more empowered. They did not choose this behavior.

Acknowledgements

My deepest and most heartfelt thanks go to:

My dad, for the dirty limericks and jokes I never understood but recall you and Uncle Jim telling while sitting on the sofa and laughing your tails off—and for bringing lingerie and red licorice underwear home to mom after your travels for work. None of which they shared with me, of course, but this light-hearted attitude made things seem less scary. The residual memory I have from this attitude was that the topic of sex could be funny too. I miss you every day, Dad.

My mom, for being mortified by dad's gifts listed above and for her sex-is-bad-or-dangerous, devout conservative, religious views, without which I'm sure I would not be doing what I do today.

Gretchen, for listening to me and playing devil's advocate for some of my topics.

Melissa, for creating my first logo and website.

Alyssa, for your podcasting partnership (and introducing me to Burning Man), which helped me to grow.

My closest friends: Heather, Jen, Marcia for your belief in me and encouragement over the years through my multitasking/grad student/divorced/mother life.

Christopher, for being an amazing example of growing up with accurate sex information and possessing a deep understanding of the power and meaning of sexuality.

Ragnar, for being my partner in crime to balance me during the toughest part of writing this and for challenging me to think more about "why" we do what we do.

My Project Heart family, for the love and encouragement to finish school and this book while simultaneously keeping me sane with a nice balance of business and pleasure. The past years were the gas that kept my tank full.

My gratitude also goes out to those who really got the ball rolling:

Shar Rednour, the original Sexy Mama, for telling me, "Honey, you gotta blog that story." Those words started me on this path—a writer who is a sexologist, a mother, AND *gasp* a sexual being.

Charlie Glickman, sex educator extraordinaire, for being my mentor and encouraging me to stick with it.

A special thank you to my personal team of advisors, my idols within the field of sex (I hope I make you proud!):

Dr. David Roth, for your advice, counsel, mentorship and making that "key" introduction.

Dr. Patti Britton, for being an amazing mentor and "earth mother" to me in this field.

Dr. Mary, for helping me prep mentally and emotionally to get "here and now."

IASHS, for providing wonderful, comprehensive sex education and the SAR process.

Dr. Ted McIlvenna, for the conviction you demonstrated toward demystifying s-e-x and for creating the often-misunderstood Institute to train an army of intelligent, empathetic, and passionate sexologists.

My IASHS family/classmates, too many to name here but you all know who you are, for your openness, honesty, and sharing your experience and expertise with me. Someone once asked me why all of my classmates were so damn beautiful. I said it was probably because you all own and live in your sexuality in an unapologetic way.

To the many sex-positive sex educators who have inspired me (in addition to the good folks above) and with whom I've become friends and admire even more: Carol Queen, Megan Andelloux, Betty Dodson, Carlin Ross, Betty Martin, and Tristan Taormino.

To more authors and educators I admire: Logan Levkoff, Judith Levine, Lou Paget, Bill Taverner, Susie Bright, Heather Corrina, and Dr. Joycelyn Elders. You do amazing work and you each have inspired me as well. Thank you!

About the Author Lanae St.John, DHS, ACS is a board-certified sexologist with the American College of Sexologists (ACS) and former professor of human sexuality at City College of San Francisco. Based in the San Francisco Bay Area, St.John uses her breadth of training and expertise to help students, clients, and readers to normalize conversations about sexuality, boundaries, respect, tolerance, and consent.

With a bachelor of science degree from the University of Wisconsin-Madison, where she focused on psychology and earned a certificate in women's studies, St.John went on to receive her Masters in Human Sexuality (MHS) and then completed her Doctorate in Human Sexuality (DHS) from the Institute for the Advanced Study of Human Sexuality. She also serves on the advisory board for the World Association of Sex Coaches (WASC), and is a member of the Society for the Scientific Study of Sexuality (SSSS), the American Association of Sex Educators, Counselors and Therapists (AASECT), and the International Society for the Study of Women's Sexual Health (ISSWSH).

A mother of two teen young women, Lanae brings her personal experience to her work as an expert on sex and parenting. Her specialty is coaching parents on the difficult task of teaching their kids about sexuality openly and honestly.

Lanae has been quoted in Forbes.com, *Huffington Post*, livestrong.com, PopSugar, AskMen, and *Women's Health Magazine*, and she's been a guest on multiple podcasts as well. Lanae lives in the San Francisco Bay Area with her two daughters and her partner Ragnar.

Endnotes

1. Greenspan, MD, L.; Deardorff, PhD, J. 2014. *The New Puberty: How to Navigate Early Development in Today's Child* [Ebook] (pp. Location 67 of 3879). Rodale Books. https://amzn.to/2Ewcnyj

2. Klepper, J. 2015. "Sin City's Missing Sexual Education: The *Daily Show* with Jon Stewart" (Video Clip) Comedy Central. http://www.cc.com/video-clips/67hgfz/the-daily-show-with-jon-stewart-sin-city-s-missing-sexual-education

3. Klepper, J. 2015. "Sin City's Missing Sexual Education: The *Daily Show* with Jon Stewart" (Video Clip) Comedy Central. http://www.cc.com/video-clips/67hgfz/the-daily-show-with-jon-stewart-sin-city-s-missing-sexual-education

4. Double X |Dream Team. 2010. http://www.slate.com/articles/double_x/doublex/2010/10/dream-team.html

5. St.John, L. 2011. "Are Men God's Gift to Women? No, the Clitoris Is." [Blog]. https://medium.com/@MamaSutra/are-men-god-s-gift-to-women-no-the-clitoris-is-a1d0be0fb945

6. St. John, L. 2011. "Sex and the Single Mother . . . and Her Kids" [Blog]. http://www.themamasutra.net/sex-and-the-single-motherand-her-kids/

7. Guttmacher Institute. 2014. *American Teens' Sexual and Reproductive Health* [Ebook]. https://www.guttmacher.org/sites/default/files/pdfs/pubs/FB-ATSRH.pdf

8. C. Lebel, C. Beaulieu. 2011. "Longitudinal Development of Human Brain Wiring Continues from Childhood into Adulthood." *Journal of Neuroscience.*

9. Taylor, M. 2012. "Tennessee Sex Ed Bans Mention of 'Gateway Sexual Behavior.'" https://abcnews.go.com/US/tennessee-governor-passes-controversial-gateway-sexual-behavior-law/story?id=16335600

10. Ryan, C.; Jethá, C. 2010. *Sex at Dawn: How We Mate, Why We Stray, and What It Means for Modern Relationships* (1): 85. New York: HarperPerennial.

11. National Center for Juvenile Justice. 2000. "Sexual Assault of Young Children as Reported to Law Enforcement: Victim, Incident, and Offender Characteristics" (p. 10). U. S. Department of Justice. https://www.bjs.gov/content/pub/pdf/saycrle.pdf

12. Sexuality Education for Children and Adolescents. 2001. PEDIATRICS, 108(2): 498-502. doi: 10.1542/peds.108.2.498

13. National Sexual Violence Resource Center. *Sexual Assault Statistics* [Ebook] (p. 1). National Sexual Violence Resource Center. http://ncdsv.org/images/sexualassaultstatistics.pdf

"14. 7 Things You Thought Wrong About Puberty." 2014. https://www.yahoo.com/lifestyle/7-things-you-thought-wrong-about-puberty-104431294272.html

15. Hay, L. 1988. *Heal Your Body: The Mental Causes for Physical Illness and the Metaphysical Way to Overcome Them* (fourth ed.). Hay House, Inc.

16. Siebel Newsom, J. 2015. "The Mask You Live In" [Video]. http://therepresentationproject.org/film/the-mask-you-live-in-film/: The Representation Project.

17. Zeff, T. 2013. *Raise an Emotionally Healthy Boy* (pp. kindle 574/2122). San Ramon, Calif.: Prana Publishing.

18. Mister Rogers defending PBS to the US Senate. 2007. [Video]. https://www.youtube.com/watch?v=yXEuEUQIP3Q

19. Utt, J. 2012. "Want the Best Sex of Your Life? Just Ask!": The Good Men Project. https://goodmenproject.com/featured-content/want-the-best-sex-of-your-life-just-ask/

20. Baczynski, M.; Mihalko, R. 2004. Cuddle Party. http://www.cuddleparty.com

21. Dean, M. 2012. "The Story of Amanda Todd." *The New Yorker*. https://www.newyorker.com/culture/culture-desk/the-story-of-amanda-todd

22. Buni, C. 2015. "The Case for Teaching Kids 'Vagina,' 'Penis,' and 'Vulva.'" *The Atlantic*. https://www.theatlantic.com/health/archive/2013/04/the- case-for-teaching-kids-vagina-penis-and-vulva/274969/

23. ABC1. 2010. Hungry Beast: Ep. 14 LABIAPLASTY (Mature) [Video]. https://vimeo.com/9924049

24. Karras, N. 2003). Petals. San Diego, CA: Crystal River Pub. Robertson, W. (2011). I'll Show You Mine. Vancouver: Show Off Books. Adachi, S., Karras, N. (2012). I [heart] my petals. Crystal River Publishing. Werner, P. (2013). 101 Vagina. Taboo Books.

25. Tabachnick, J., Klein, A. 2011. *A Reasoned Approach: Reshaping Sex Offender Policy to Prevent Child Sexual Abuse* [Ebook] (p. 14). Beaverton, Oregon: Association for the Treatment of Sexual Abusers. http://www.atsa.com/pdfs/ppReasonedApproach.pdf

"26. A Lesson in Sexual Abuse Prevention from Oprah Winfrey's Interview with Matt Sandusky." 2014. [Blog]. https://www.sexwiseparent.com/2014/07/23/a-lesson-in-sexual-abuse-prevention-from-oprah-winfreys-interview-with-matt-sandusky/

27. AMC. 2014. *Mad Men*, S4 Ep5 THE CHRYSANTHEMUM AND THE SWORD [Video]. https://www.amc.com/shows/mad-men/season-4/episode-05-the-chrysanthemum-and-the-sword

28. A judgmental term meaning someone having more sex than you are.

29. Smiler, A. 2013. "Consent 102: Clarifying the Gray Spaces:" The Good Men Project. https://goodmenproject.com/featured-content/andrew-smiler-consent-102-clarifying-the-gray-spaces/

30. Mister Rogers defending PBS to the US Senate. 2007. [Video]. https://www.youtube.com/watch?v=yXEuEUQIP3Q

31. National Center for Juvenile Justice. 2000. Sexual Assault of Young Children as Reported to Law Enforcement: Victim, Incident, and Offender Characteristics (p. 10). US Department of Justice. https://www.bjs.gov/content/pub/pdf/saycrle.pdf

32. Glickman, C. 2016. "Taking No for An Answer" [Blog]. http://www.makesexeasy.com/taking-answer/

33. Richmond, T. 2013. "Business Selling Snuggles Raises Suspicion in Madison, Wis." *The Washington Post*. https://www.washingtonpost.com/politics/business-selling-snuggles-raises-suspicion-in-madison-wis/2013/12/08/08c8e098-605c-11e3-94ad-004fefa61ee6_story.html?noredirect=on&utm_term=.501f212702ff

34. Morin, J. 1995. *The Erotic Mind: Unlocking the Inner Sources of Sexual Passion and Fulfillment*. (1st ed.). (p. 141). New York: Harper Perennial.

35. "If She's Not Having Fun You Have to Stop." 2009. [Blog]. https://yesmeansyesblog.wordpress.com/2009/10/29/if-shes-not-having-fun-you-have-to-stop/

36. Lee, V., and Keller, M. 2015. "Former Stanford University Swimmer Faces Rape Charges." https://abc7news.com/news/former-stanford-swimmer-faces-rape-charges/500747/.

37. Barchenger, S., and Garrison, J. 2015. "Vanderbilt Rape Trial: Defendants Found Guilty on All Charges. https://www.usatoday.com/story/sports/ncaaf/sec/2015/01/27/vanderbilt-players-verdict-guilty-rape-vandenburg-batey/22430567/

38. Schweber, J., and Schweber, N. 2012. "Rape Case Unfolds Online and Divides Steubenville." https://www.nytimes.

com/2012/12/17/sports/high-school-football-rape-case-unfolds-online-and-divides-steubenville-ohio.html

39. New American Standard Bible. 1995 (pp. 1 Corinthians 6:19). The Lockman Foundation.

40. Sanghani, R. 2015. "Sex, Porn and Mythical genitalia: Girls at Single-Sex Schools Aren't That Innocent."https://www.telegraph.co.uk/women/womens-life/11477220/Sex-porn-and-genitalia-Girls-at-single-sex-schools-arent-innocent.html

41. Nolte, D. 1972. "Children Learn What They Live." http://www.empowermentresources.com/info2/childrenlearn-long_version.html

42. Manaster, H. 2012. "He's Not My Boyfriend, He's My Buddy. [Blog]. https://superheroprincess.wordpress.com/2012/06/12/hes-not-my-boyfriend-hes-my-buddy/#more-1600

43. Griffin, L. 2011. "The Upside to Boy-Girl Friendships." https://www.psychologytoday.com/us/blog/field-guide-families/201112/the-upside-boy-girl-friendships

44. Wallace, A. 2015. "Opinion: It's a girl!' Not so fast…" https://www.cnn.com/2015/03/17/opinions/avery-wallace-teen/index.html

45. The Spectrum. 2019. https://www.thetrevorproject.org/about/programs-services/coming-out-as-you/the-spectrum/#sm.0001ki7v07fglewosdo21xnbvjl6d

46. Tillerman, S. 2018. The Genderbread Person v4. https://www.itspronouncedmetrosexual.com/2018/10/the-genderbread-person-v4/

47. Social Construct. 2019. Merriam Webster. https://www.merriam-webster.com/dictionary/social%20construct

48. Adolescent Sexual Orientation. 2008. *Paediatrics and Child Health*, 13 (7): 619-30.

49. Filipovic, J. 2013. "'Purity' Culture: Bad for Women, Worse for Survivors of Sexual Assault." https://www.theguardian.com/commentisfree/2013/may/09/elizabeth-smart-purity-culture-shames-survivors-sexual-assault

50. Lovett, I., and Nagourney, A. 2014. "Video Rant, Then Deadly Rampage in California Town." https://www.nytimes.com/2014/05/25/us/california-drive-by-shooting.html

51. Wiseman, R. 2002. *Queen Bees and Wannabes.* New York: Three Rivers Press.

52. *Seinfeld* "The Implant". 1993. https://www.imdb.com/title/tt0697711/

53. Mean Girls Clip 2 / "Standing in Front of the Mirror." 2012. [Video]. https://www.youtube.com/watch?v=ZZDQYVU8o9M

54. Beauty Pressure. 2007. https://www.youtube.com/watch?v=Ei6JvK0W60I

55. Dove Ad. 2007. https://www.youtube.com/watch?v=RWNYndqFTR4

56. Steinberg, L. 2011. "Parent-Child Relationships: Infancy, Toddlerhood, Preschool, School Age, Adolescence, Adults." http://psychology.jrank.org/pages/472/Parent-Child-Relationships.html

57. Kindlon, D., and Thompson, M. 2009. *Raising Cain: Protecting the Emotional Life of Boys.* New York: Random House Publishing Group.

58. Chu, J. 2014. *When Boys Become Boys: Development, Relationships, and Masculinity.* New York: New York University Press.

59. Stranger Than Fiction: Hugs Banned in Schools. 2012. http://www.aaeteachers.org/index.php/blog/852-stranger-than-fiction-hugs-banned-in-schools

60. Resnick, S. 2012. *The Heart of Desire: Keys to the Pleasures of Love.* Hoboken: John Wiley and Sons Ltd.

61. Keltner, D. 2010. "Hands On Research: The Science of Touch." https://greatergood.berkeley.edu/article/item/hands_on_research

62. Lehmiller, J. 2014. "The Power of Touch: The Crucial Role of Physical Intimacy in Relationships" [Blog]. https://www.lehmiller.com/blog/2014/9/11/the-power-of-touch-the-crucial-role-of-physical-intimacy-in-relationship-success

63. Sensate Focus | SexInfo Online. 2012. http://www.soc.ucsb.edu/sexinfo/article/sensate-focus

64. Suebsaeng, A. 2013. "The Evan Rachel Wood Oral Sex Scene the MPAA Doesn't Want You to See." https://www.motherjones.com/politics/2013/12/shia-labeouf-evan-rachel-wood-oral-sex-scene-mpaa-charlie-countryman/

65. Jehl, D. 1994. "Surgeon General Forced to Resign by White House." https://www.nytimes.com/1994/12/10/us/surgeon-general-forced-to-resign-by-white-house.html

66. CBS. 2008. "Weeds—Masturbation" [Video]. https://www.youtube.com/watch?v=GJkEwbVdcQY

67. Anatomy of the Clitoris. 2012. [Image]. http://www.drjack.co.uk/wp-content/uploads/2012/09/Anatomy_of_the_clitoris1.jpg

68. Bright, S. 2008. *Mommy's Little Girl: On Sex, Motherhood, Porn, and Cherry Pi*e (p. 21). Santa Cruz, CA: Bright Stuff.

69. "'Because It Feels Good': The Starting Point for Talking to Kids About Sex." (2011). [Blog]. https://goodmenproject.com/sex-relationships/because-it-feels-good-the-starting-point-for-talking-to-kids-about-sex/

70. Hite, S. 2003. *The Hite Report: A Nationwide Study of Female Sexuality.* New York: Seven Stories Press.

71. Zilbergeld, B. 1999. *The New Male Sexuality: The Truth about Men, Sex, and Pleasure* (p. 15). New York: Bantam Doubleday Dell Publishing Group.

72. Zilbergeld, B. (1999). The New Male Sexuality: The Truth about Men, Sex, and Pleasure (p. 15). New York: Bantam Doubleday Dell Publishing Group

73. Ogas, O., and Gaddam, S. 2011. *Billion Wicked Thoughts.* New York: Penguin Group (USA) Inc.

74. James, E.L. 2011. *Fifty Shades of Grey* (*Fifty Shades Trilogy* #1). United States: The Writer's Coffee Shop.

75. Advocates for Youth. 2007. *The Truth About Abstinence-Only Programs* [Ebook]. Washington, DC. https://futureofsexed.org/storage/advfy/documents/fsabstinenceonly.pdfs

76. Santelli, J., Ott, M., Lyon, M., Rogers, J., Summers, D., and Schleifer, R. 2006. "Abstinence and Abstinence-Only Education: A Review of US Policies and Programs." *Journal of Adolescent Health.* 38(1): 72-81. doi: 10.1016/j.jadohealth.2005.10.006

77. Santelli, J., Ott, M., Lyon, M., Rogers, J., Summers, D., and Schleifer, R. 2006. Abstinence and abstinence-only education: A review of US policies and programs. Journal Of Adolescent Health, 38(1), 72-81. doi: 10.1016/j.jadohealth.2005.10.006

78. Finer, L., and Philbin, J. 2013. "Sexual Initiation, Contraceptive Use, and Pregnancy Among Young Adolescents." PEDIATRICS, 131(5): 886-891. doi: 10.1542/peds.2012-3495

79. Finer, L., and Philbin, J. (2013). Sexual Initiation, Contraceptive Use, and Pregnancy Among Young Adolescents. PEDIATRICS, 131(5), 886-891. doi: 10.1542/peds.2012-3495

80. Lagina, N., and Whittaker, A. 2010. *Parent-Child Communication: Promoting Sexually Healthy Youth* [Ebook]. Washington, DC: Advocates for Youth. https://www.advocates-foryouth.org/wp-content/uploads/storage//advfy/documents/parent%20child%20communication%202010.pdf

81. Walt Disney Pictures. 1991. *Beauty and the Beast.* [Film]. Hollywood.

82. Sexual Self-Confidence. 2012. http://reidaboutsex.com/sexual-self-confidence-2/

83. Hess, A. 2013. "How Does internet Porn Affect Teens? New Study Says: We Have No Idea." https://slate.com/human-interest/2013/05/internet-porn-study-the-effect-of-pornography-on-kids-and-teens-remains-inconclusive.html

84. Finer, L. 2007. "Trends in Premarital Sex in the United States, 1954–2003." Public Health Reports, 122(1): 73-78. doi: 10.1177/003335490712200110

85. Gallop, C. 2009. "Launched Today in Teta: MakeLoveNotPorn.tv." https://blog.ted.com/launched-today-in-beta-makelovenotporn-tv/

86. Levine, J., and Elders, J. 2002. *Harmful to Minors: The Perils of Protecting Children from Sex.* Minneapolis: University of Minnesota Press.

87. Levine, J. (2002). *Harmful to Minors: The Perils of Protecting Children from Sex.* Minneapolis: University of Minnesota Press.

88. Sorella, L. 2016. "Top 7 Myths About Crossdressers and Transgender Women." https://feminizationsecrets.com/transgender-crossdressing-myths

89. Herbenick, D., Reece, M., Schick, V., Sanders, S., Dodge, B., and Fortenberry, J. 2010. "Sexual Behavior in the United States: Results from a National Probability Sample of Men and Women Ages 14–94." *The Journal of Sexual Medicine*, 7, 255-265. doi: 10.1111/j.1743-6109.2010.02012.x

90. Petrosino, A., Turpin-Petrosino, C., and Buehler, J. 2002. "*Scared Straight* and Other Juvenile Awareness Programs for Preventing Juvenile Delinquency." The ANNALS of the American Academy of Political and Social Science, (2). doi: 10.1177/0002716203254693

91. The White House: President Barack Obama. 2014. A Renewed Call to Action to End Rape and Sexual Assault. Washington, DC: Obama Administration.

92. 1 is 2 Many PSA: 60 Second. 2014. https://obamawhitehouse.archives.gov/1is2many

93. Lang, A. 2010. "Birds + Bees + Kids: The Basics" [Video]. BBK Video.

94. Brown, B. 2012. "Listening to Shame" [Video]. https://www.ted.com/talks/brene_brown_listening_to_shame

CPSIA information can be obtained
at www.ICGtesting.com
Printed in the USA
FSHW020750270320
68531FS